David Rozzell served as a combat soldier in 1967 and 1968 during the Vietnam War, which serves as the explosive backdrop for his extraordinary memoir, *Troubled Sleep*. *Troubled Sleep* is, by turns, a brilliant journalistic tour de force of Rozzell's experiences in that surreal theatre; but, perhaps most poignantly a searingly candid account of the trauma he internalized, was forced to heroically repress during the war, then tote home with him – his "blistered soul," as he terms it – and courageously and unimaginably keep those demons of war at bay for the rest of his life. This is a harrowing book, but more than anything an absolutely necessary one. Its stories are rendered beautifully – with finesse and abundant, often deadpan humor – by a narrator (Rozzell) whom readers will trust, admire, and even fall in love with. Rozzell is a born writer, a storyteller of profound mettle, magnanimous spirit, with an inimitable voice at once comforting, wry, warm, inspiring, believable, and quintessentially human and humane. *Troubled Sleep* is another utterly invaluable book to put on your shelf about the Vietnam War. David Rozzell is a wonder.

–Joseph Bathanti, North Carolina Poet Laureate (2012-14) & 2016 Charles George VA Medical Center Writer-in-Residence

TROUBLED SLEEP

TROUBLED SLEEP

DAVID ROZZELL

REDHAWK
PUBLICATIONS

Troubled Sleep
Copyright © 2025 David Rozzell

All rights reserved. No part of this publication may be reproduced, distributed, or transmitted in any form or by any means, including photocopying, recording, or other electronic or mechanical methods, without the prior written permission of the publisher, except in the case of brief quotations embodied in critical reviews and specific other noncommercial uses permitted by copyright law.
For permission requests, write to the publisher, addressed
"Attention: Permissions Coordinator," at the address below.

ISBN: 978-1-959346-83-8 (Paperback)
Library of Congress Control Number: 2024000000

Book Layout and Cover: Erin Mann

Cover Image Source: James K. F. Dung, Photograph of helicopters airlifting soldiers to a new staging area in South Vietnam, 1966, National Archives and Records Administration

Printed in the United States of America.
First printing edition 2025

Redhawk Publications
The Catawba Valley Community College Press
2550 Hwy 70 SE
Hickory NC 28602l
https://redhawkpublications.com

To Judy, David's amazing wife, who brought horses,
history, travel, and music back into his life.

*David Thomas Rozzell died on October 22, 2022.
Dedication was made by his loving sisters,
Terri, Carol, and Pegg.
Thank you, Judy, for loving our big brother and
for being his champion.*

I stand amid the roar
Of a surf-tormented shore,
And I hold within my hand
Grains of the golden sand —
How few! yet how they creep
Through my fingers to the deep,
While I weep — while I weep!
O God! Can I not grasp
Them with a tighter clasp?
O God! can I not save
One from the pitiless wave?

–Edgar Allen Poe

TABLE OF CONTENTS

Introduction	11
What Healing Looks Like	13
Prologue	14
Pre-Flight	15
Arrival	17
Replacement Company	21
Slim	23
Top	27
Carl	31
Thunder 1	35
Dream	39
Banana	41
LT	43
Ohio	49
Captain Red	55
Golf	61
Eagle Flight	65
Duke	71
Monk	77
Herc	79
Yearling	87
Bob	89
Over the Hill	91
Word	93
Cobra	95
Water	97
Firebase Raising	105
Cat	107
Christmas Eve	109
Christmas Morning	111
The Navy	115

Skipper	117
Retreat	119
To the Cav	121
Purple	125
Jake	129
Johnny	139
Aaron	149
Pistol	151
Red	157
The Dean	159
Braced	163
Kid	165
Rabies	167
Don	169
X-ray Boss	171
Bugs	173
Food	175
Runs	177
DJ	179
Mustache	181
Extraction	185
Z	189
Major Stone	195
Patton	199
The Gaze	201
Final Exam	203
Home	207
Acknowledgments	210
Uncle David	212
Author Bio	213
Permissions	214

INTRODUCTION

My name is David Rozzell. I was a combat medic with the 1st Infantry, Vietnam, 1969. When I came home, I experienced problems fitting into civilian life. I spent thirty-five years believing I did not have problems, but the war and its horrors stayed within me. Five years ago, Dr. Bruce Kelly, my primary care doctor at the Oteen VA Medical Center, invited me to join a creative writing program for veterans with PTSD. As part of this great group of veterans, I have been able to share the feelings I had while in combat. The other members of the group accepted the feelings as normal. Normal to us. I have been fortunate to be part of this talented, caring group and have watched the lives of many men get easier. They have made life much easier for me.

With the help of Dr. Joseph Bathanti, North Carolina Poet Laureate and the group's co-founder, I have learned to accept my frustration. I live easier but know the anxiety will never fully go away.

This is a collection of stories of random human beings thrown into a life-altering situation. The situation was war. The war in South Vietnam, to be specific, and the years 1969 and 1970, to be exact. I entered the war as a twenty-three-year-old aspiring golf professional after graduating in 1968 from North Carolina State University with a turf management and ornamental horticulture degree. Rather than applying this hard-won knowledge to golf courses in need of a young, promising professional, I spent most of my efforts the following year in an unsuccessful quest to avoid the draft.

By the time I met the characters you will read about in the following pages, I had spent eight weeks of June and July 1969 in 90 degree heat at Fort Campbell, Kentucky, boot camp. In August, I was flown into San Antonio, Texas, where I was greeted with 104 degree heat. By Thanksgiving, I had completed the U.S. Army educational requirements to serve as a combat medic. The training and knowledge were barely kindergarten for the education to come. In combat situations, the real medic job—in addition to keeping the men in your charge alive—included making sure the men took their malaria pills, wrote home to mother, kept their feet dry. Later, in more intense experiences, I would learn to close wounds and apply tourniquets. The last and most painful job was the placement of deceased men into body bags, wiring a plain manila tag with the man's core information firmly to the toe, and sending his remains to Graves Registration. I did not want to send any soldier home in this condition, but I was not going to send them home with the wrong identity.

There was a lot of off-duty time, and I learned to fill much of it with the study of people. I have mental records of actions and conversations I was a part of. I did not get close to the men of any group I was assigned to in combat. It was enough to know the men I could most depend on and make sure they knew they could depend on me.

I don't know what became of the people I have written about since coming home from Vietnam. That is one of the sad things about the work I did—there was no follow-up or contact afterward. Long term, I have no idea if the men I treated lived, suffered permanently from their wounds, or died. I know that most of them were as ill-prepared for war as I was.

These days, I'm a horse farmer. I went back to school and got a master's degree in counseling, hoping to make some sense of where I'd been. It is sad that after so many years, I still have questions, just questions and more questions, and these stories.

WHAT HEALING LOOKS LIKE

To drop the rusty 8-feet length steel chain
which holds the ring of idle keys
just out of reach of my tired left hand.

To know I am no longer responsible
for remembering which triple-plated copper padlock
keeps the anger trigger within from escaping
and which bone-toothed key keeps that lock fast
and the beast behind its flimsy door at bay.

To know which key tightens the screen door
and works so pitifully, yet is responsible
for slowing the night horror ghosts and ghouls.

To release my death grip from the key
that controls the lock, which keeps the higher windows
closed to slow the cold fears which scream
by the loose-fitting frame of those windows
and my being tensed and prepped for fight.

To push with confidence the stubborn turnstile
that bars me from any seat except
the absolute back row spot nearest to the aisle.

To gently turn and relax my grip
on the icy door knob
behind which potential friends await.

To walk airily, quietly, peacefully,
hearing the clang of the chain and keys,
knowing they are real,
but do not control my soul.

–David Rozzell, 2017

PROLOGUE

While I was in Vietnam, I sent many letters home. As I look back at the few letters still in circulation, I realize I wrote of general things and never mentioned any of the blood and guts that came with my involvement in the war.

Where my grandfather Frank was concerned, I was not as shy. He answered with equal candor. Shortly after the first real shootout, I described to Frank in some detail the smell of gunpowder, the whiz of lead around my head, and the excitement of my coworkers.

After confessing some amount of personal fear, I ended the letter, "I was so scared that I didn't know whether to pee or wind my watch."

My grandmother Louisa, Frank's wife, was a Savage. That was her family name, and she took it to heart. Louisa used the watch-winding saying often, and I knew it would make them smile.

Time and the war continued. I got more hardened to the day-to-day battle grind.

A month or so later, I got a small package in the mail call. I loved mail call. I tore into the brown wrapping paper, not really caring what it was. It was a package, and it was from home.

Inside the package, I found a watch and a letter from my grandfather. The letter had the general news about the bean and corn crop, but the meat and the potatoes came at the end. "Bud, this watch is battery-powered. There is no need to worry about winding it. When you get into the tight spots, just shoot the son of a bitch."

PRE-FLIGHT

IN MID NOVEMBER of 1969, I was at home in Black Mountain, North Carolina, packing to go to the war zone in Vietnam. A couple of days before my plane was to leave, Dad and I drove to the East Tennessee mountain coal mining town of Bon Air to visit my grandfather Frank.

My dad's people had been in Bon Air, Tennessee, and the coal mines in one capacity or another for three generations. I knew the stories and had been shown the towns and countrysides. My dad had gone to college after the war and took an engineering vocation. If he hadn't, I would have also been part of the Tennessee mountain community.

Frank was the male family member most suited for war and combat. He was also the most frustrated since he was too young to fight in WWI and too old to fight in WWII. His father was one of the original Tennessee Volunteers who fought in the Spanish-American War. His son, my dad, had seen combat as a B-17 pilot in WWII, and now I was going to the latest conflict.

We had a pleasant visit. Frank let me shoot all the guns he had and offered to let me carry the .45 Colt revolver and the .45-70 carbine rifle his father had used to fight the Spanish. I was firing his .45 cal Colt revolver, and he could not resist turning one of his favorite tricks on me. The first three shells contained standard powder loads—the third he had put in a black powder round he saved for such occasions. The kick of that round knocked my arm over my head, and the smoke blinded us all for 3 minutes. I thanked him for the offer but assured him I would be provided with more up-to-date equipment.

My grandmother cooked nonstop, preparing for the few hours we were there. She was a wonderful mountain cook and would never take no for an answer to a few pieces of pecan pie or fried chicken. I would never have hurt her feelings. She was also good at dominating any conversation and kept the visit on a lighter plane than it would have otherwise been.

As we were leaving, Frank came to the car out of my grandmother's hearing range but not Dad's. He told me not to be concerned about the prospect of not coming home from the war. He said for me to be brave, as was the family tradition, and that, as a precaution and just in case something did happen, he had purchased a cemetery plot next to the one where my great-grandfather was buried in Bon Air. It was a sincere gesture, I am sure. But the conversation ended quietly on that note, and Dad quickly drove us toward the interstate.

ARRIVAL

AN EARLY AFTERNOON mid-November day in 1969—the Tiger Airline jet I shared with some two-hundred soldiers made a soft landing at the U.S. military Army base in Bien Hoa, South Vietnam. We had been elbow-to-elbow in the belly of that big sheet metal bird for eleven hours and knew nothing except that we were all going to war.

The plane rolled to a stop, and we stepped meekly into a new world. The landing area was not how I pictured the airfield of *the greatest Army in the history of the world*. It was imposing as a large flat area of earth undisturbed by vegetation, but the buildings reminded me more of large cotton or grain storage and shipping buildings than military structures. The roofs were corrugated metal, walls of unpainted concrete blocks. Fully half of the roofs covered only concrete floors.

We were greeted by the strong, sweet smell of freshly pressed and finished asphalt. The new asphalt was lightly covered by reddish, sandy-colored dust, much as an early fall sprinkle of snow would cover the courthouse parking lot of any county seat in North Georgia. The older patches of pavement were completely covered with dust except for the lines left by various vehicles. Any movement of truck, plane, or man stirred clouds of the offensive dust, which settled quietly on any stationary surface.

The sky was cloudless and endless. There were no mountains or hills to give us a ground boundary. The temperature was 112 degrees. With the unfiltered sun, I could not have seen a horizon if there had been one.

After that welcome, we were greeted by an army of military men who were excited to see us and anxious to get us checked off

David Rozzell

any one of many lists and get us organized into groups headed to meet with other groups of soldiers in the name of processing.

The process men were a loud bunch. I guessed they were all practicing their command voices. There were too many of them for the job at hand, but they all seemed satisfied with their individual performances. Their chatter, accompanied by the noise of various jets, helicopters, and trucks, proved a sharp contrast to the quiet of my deplaning companions. I was not comforted.

All our belongings were packed neatly and firmly into the standard Army-issued duffle bags. We had our name and military ID number stenciled in black on the side of the bag. As we were climbing from the plane, our bags were dumped with no respect into a heap from the belly of that plane. In the short time it took us to get from the ladder leading off the front of the plane to the collection site, the duffle bags collected their first coating of dust. The squad leader who claimed our little processing group put us into an almost military line of twos, had us shoulder our bags, and led us toward one of the large open buildings. As we approached the corner of the building, our commander signaled us to halt. We dropped our bags respectfully and watched a company of uniformed Vietnamese men march past. It was our first sight of the local Army. My first thought was that they were a local high school ROTC unit. They had new, well-fitted uniforms, but I would have guessed the average age was thirteen. Our leader assured us we were viewing the South Vietnam Regular Army and that we should refer to them as ARVN.

We stood silently watching the military parade of ARVN. We were here to support these men. I hoped, without much conviction, that we were not watching the best soldiers this country had. After the dust settled behind the ARVN parade, we shouldered our duffle bags and marched smartly to a waiting school bus refashioned to transport American troops. The bus had a fresh coat of olive drab paint, the swing-out stop signs had been removed, the wheels had been painted a flat black, and 1" square galvanized chicken wire had been riveted to cover the glass windows. The windows were open to provide some small amount of air movement in the otherwise unbearable heat inside the bus. One of the loudest of the processing soldiers told our little group that the wire was to stop grenades from being tossed into the bus as it drove through the crowded streets.

The bus driver and the two processing men with him carried sidearms. They did not appear concerned about the grenade-tossing enemy. I sat by one of the open chicken-wire-covered windows, mid-bus and off-side. I also took a close look at the thin sheet metal covering of the bus. It was clear to me that the wall between me and the street was not going to turn any serious bullet. The image of being protected by sheet metal and chicken wire struck me as very funny, then as very frightening.

Our bus trip covered about two miles through what must have been the outskirts of Bien Hoa. I could not push hard enough to make it end nor hold back strongly enough to keep it from finding the next intersection, which meant contact with a new set of cars, trucks, and maybe the enemy. At least one of the crossroads at which we stopped to give right-of-way to a convoy of locals had open fields on my side of the bus. The fields were full of grade-school children running after each other, playing tag games I had played when I was that age. They were laughing and unaffected by us. The kids were acting as happy and normal as any group of children I had ever seen. I missed home. I searched the group and the surrounding area for signs of war and terror. If there was any worry, aggression, or fear alive in that playground, I could not find it.

The bus pulled away from that intersection and belched a dark cloud of moist diesel vapors in my face. The street we merged onto filled my nose with fumes from a fresh coat of asphalt, and a soft breeze sprinkled every surface near me with another jacket of warm, chalky dust.

I am not sure if I was more surprised or relieved when the bus drove through the sandbagged pillars protecting the gatepost and gatekeepers of the processing facility. When the transport stopped, and the diesel-fume dust settled softly in front of us, we dismounted gracefully, considering the awkward duffel bags, which were as wide as the aisle and doorway of the bus. The escort assigned to find us sleeping quarters marched us in circles for a while and then dismissed us to his first assistant, who herded us into the back corner of an open building. With the addition of clean walls, windows, and a few rows of benches, it could have been the assembly hall or sanctuary of any Christian church I had attended. Our particular sleeping area was defined by a waist-high wall of sandbags and two close-order rows of military break-down cots. Each cot was covered with a woven wool blanket of olive drab color, a feather pillow with case, and a light covering of dust.

    As a parting gift, our usher told us to "find a bunk, put your bag under it, and report to the parade ground at the north entrance in fifteen minutes." By now, I was beginning to see that there were a lot of soldiers doing things other than marching through the jungle killing the enemy.

REPLACEMENT COMPANY

A BUGLE BLAST of reveille woke me the next morning, my first full morning in the war zone. The rudeness of the greeting assured me that I had been asleep for some period of time the first short night. The bugle call was my standard morning welcome since I became a soldier, but this one was louder, the pitch higher, the tone bolder, and the decay longer than the others.

The welcoming committee was as large as the host that met us at the airport. I did not recognize any of the men, but their command voices were the same, and their orders clipped and cold. At 0700 hours, we assembled on the parade ground outside our barracks. The loudest member of our leadership informed us that we were now members of Replacement Company 441 and that until we had orders to a permanent company, we were to report to formation here every morning at 0700 and every afternoon at 1600. Furthermore, failure to do so would subject us "to Summary Court-Martial."

The loud-mouthed leader stepped back, and his assistant moved boldly to the front of us. With a command voice that squeaked like Kermit the Frog, he read the names of each man expected to be present in our formation. The bold human presented orders to those of us assigned new outfits and repeated the warning to the rest that we were expected in the next formation.

The men of the little band I was thrown in with were all new to war. When you have no idea what is happening, it is easier to be led. The formation was alive with stage whispers. "Yesterday, the 25th lost a machine gunner only two days short of going home." "The 1st Cav moved a whole company to the DMZ." "The Big Red One is going home in December." We had heard most of these unit names. Every unit name had a story to go with it. None of the stories inspired peace or comfort.

The man in front of me was called out to report immediately to the 1st Cav. Then, the next three men called were assigned to the same outfit. My immediate thought was *that outfit must be getting a bunch of men killed.* It somehow did not occur to me that the 1st Cav might be replacing men who were finishing their tour of duty. At that time, I would have been as likely to believe they were replacing men who were being excused to go on a church picnic.

My name was eventually called, and I was informed that I "was not yet permanently assigned." That sentence was repeated to most of the men in our formation, and a few were conspicuous because of their absence. A new leader moved to our front and matter-of-factly said, "If you have gotten assignments, move to the rear of the formation for your paperwork. The rest of you follow me to In-Country Orientation."

SLIM

AT 0800, MY third day in the War Zone, I found myself and a large and quiet collection of men dressed in newly U.S. Army-issued olive drab jungle uniforms awaiting orders at a desert-like rifle range similar to the base rifle ranges of Texas, Kentucky, South Carolina, and Georgia. We were a formation of Army personnel of every stripe: infantry, cook, clerk, artillery, medic. They were all new faces to me and to each other, and we were all there to be familiarized with the M16 rifle.

I had never held or even seen an M16, an M79 grenade launcher, an M60 machine gun, or, for that matter, any of the other weapons on display there, much less fired one. In the time near what was allotted to learn such, I did manage to get the basic assembly of the 16. That task accomplished, I randomly fired a few rounds at some non-functioning pop-up targets with no illusion that I hit one or even scared one. For my efforts, I was awarded the expert marksmanship medal.

During the field dressing lessons—taking the M16 apart, cleaning, oiling, and putting the thing back together without extra parts—I noticed the man beside me idly playing a game of mumble-typeg with his weathered knife. That game pegged him firmly as a farm kid. I had spent many hours flipping my knife from different heights and body parts, trying to get more revolutions and still have it land in the designated spot and stand for the required count of ten.

I knew the guy was a medic and that he also had orders to report to the 1st Infantry along with me. That proved reason enough to make us travel companions. His lack of interest in lessons about guns and killing did bother me. I spent too much time watching the man's inaction and wondering why the heck the officer in charge was unconcerned. No one other than me even looked at the man.

When the work of getting trained ended for the day, I got serious about finding out what was going on with this dude. He shot me an answer that he thought closed the discussion: "I'm a conscientious objector."

To my curious little mind, that was simply a beginning. He was indeed a farm boy from one of the big farms in Utah. He had done the farm boy stuff I had—milked cows, ridden horses and young bulls, and I'm sure did better. He drove tractors, baled hay, and logged timber with a draft team. With his dad and two older brothers, he had hunted whatever game was in season. He knew the habits of lake and stream fish. He had done well in school and possessed a respectable curveball and a winning record pitching for his high school baseball team his senior year. His baseball coach gave him the name he carried to war: Slim.

§

After much too long a cross-examination, I got the answer I was hunting. I was still not satisfied. The C.O. status was granted routinely to members of the Mennonite Church, and Slim was indeed a member. His family and neighbors were members and had been members for several generations. I never found him to be ashamed of the fact nor proud of it.

Slim and I were travelers on the same road. We spent most of the next week together. We stood together in long, hot, dust-laden lines to eat bad food, get painful haircuts, pick up uniforms that may or may not prove to be the size advertised, and be issued boots with labels that should have said "one size fits all."

We sat in large groups of new arrivals, listening to medical people explain the evils of loose women and unprotected sex, the dangers of mosquito-borne disease, and the importance of regular dental care. The military people explained the importance of aiming your weapon low cause "Charlie" was not going to stand and wave his arms.

Then, the Army religious corp representative went on to explain the importance of maintaining a strong relationship with God. He was followed by an overdressed political officer, over-impressed with his importance, who assured us that we were personally "stamping out aggression wherever he reared his ugly head." We were ready now for combat.

In the time between formation and meals, Slim and I pitched a baseball Slim had lifted from the depths of a supply room somewhere. It is a mindless activity, and, except for the inferior conditions of our gloves and the pain my ribs held after being slammed by a hard curve Slim got by my glove, it was a welcome and peaceful time. Some of the best memories of my earlier childhood centered around a game of pitch with my father.

After learning all we had to at in-processing, Slim and I caught a jeep to the 1st Division's Medic Company. We reported and were told that the first sergeant was away for the day. The clerk pointed us in the general direction of the enlisted men's barrack tent and assured us there would be empty bunks and people to tell us what to do. He strongly suggested we report back to him in the morning.

The baseball and glove had somehow attached itself to Slim's duffle bag, so we resumed his postwar preparation for a career in the major leagues. We tested the limits of the company area and listened with fear to the war stories that every GI seemed to have on the tip of his tongue. Sometime during that day, Slim became a smoker.

TOP

THE NEXT MORNING was not as relaxed. Top, the first sergeant, was back in the company area, and everyone was moving wide open. Top took Slim and me by the scruff and dragged us through his personal version of combat field orientation. He told us we would be leaving early tomorrow morning for base camp Thunder I to join Company A. A Company was commanded by Captain Campbell, and we were to address him as SIR. Top announced proudly that Capt. Campbell, who was now midway through his second combat tour as a company commander, was "the best company commander in The Big Red One."

Slim and I would be assigned our platoon for each combat mission and report to the officer in charge of that particular platoon. We were never to be disrespectful to any officer or non-commissioned officer or do anything else to bring reproach to Top's name. Top was not a big specimen of humanity. He was not especially tall, not heavily muscled. He did not sport facial hair, nor was his dark, straight hair too closely cut. In any other setting, Top would pass for a typical, average person. In this company area, he was master of all he surveyed.

With his pep talk complete, Top double-timed us to the supply room. The supply room was a large tent with a hastily fabricated wooden front and two doors secured by a lock, which was ornamental at best. The supply room underling was a buck sergeant with long legs and a wiry body that, along with the hunkered back and lack of conversational skill, brought to my mind the young men I had seen walking the low mountains of Eastern Tennessee.

Top had Slim and me open and dump the contents of our duffel bags. He and Mr Tennessee sorted through our stuff with intensity and more speed and dexterity than the bum who went through the dumpster behind the 7-11 at home. They pitched anything with a pleasant odor, like deodorant, after-shave lotion, shaving cream, mouthwash, toothpaste, and foot powders, into a large pile of like items. Top grabbed the gas mask I had been careful to keep in my eyesight. I had misplaced one in basic training and paid a heavy price to get it returned. He slung the expensive thing casually aside, saying, "Won't need one of those stupid things."

Slim had made it through all our in-processing and new-in-country retraining with an air mattress. The mattress was of durable nylon construction and OD in color. I had never seen such a thing but naively took his word that it was Regular Army. Top had other ideas. We were in his army now. The mattress went harshly into a small pile, and Slim got a look from Top, which prevented any discussion on the matter.

The censor from hell tore into our clothing. We had invested many a blazing hot hour in long lines to collect pants, shirts, boxer shorts, boots that actually fit, socks, and soft OD undershirts. The inspectors sorted everything except what we wore into stacks of similar but abused like items. And, as if we were not capable of keeping up with our duffel bags, Mr Tennessee took them too.

Top handed us each a metal backpack frame with a canvas kit filled with medical supplies. The frame also had an empty canvas pouch below the med stuff, in which we were to carry necessities like C-rations, poncho and liner, and extra ammo. Top believed everything else a man carried was in the way.

At this point, I got the impression that Top had lost interest in us. He bluntly dismissed us with, "Get over to the mess tent, then report to headquarters at 1600." He was single-handedly fighting a war, and we were not being much help.

Slim and I reported at 1600. Top was impatiently holding six sheets of freshly-processed DoD forms. He had us sign the one with our name and serial number affixed. With our signatures, he held proof he had fulfilled all his responsibilities concerning us and was sending two fully-prepared and fully-equipped, if also fully innocent, military medics into mortal combat. What could possibly go wrong?

CARL

SLIM AND I reported to the formation area at 0700, as ordered. We had our backpacks and steel headgear and were ready to move out. Top was there to make sure we reported, and, satisfied, he vanished.

As soon as Top was out of sight, a dust-coated enlisted man stepped down from a deuce-and-a-half Army truck that had been parked in the sparsely graveled lot. The guy from the truck was the driver who was to take us to Thunder 1 and combat. He was 5'6" tall and had a classic pear-shaped body. His hair was in bad need of barbering, and his mustache would have done any walrus proud. None of the man's uniform pieces fit right. He wore Coke bottle glasses, which were clearly not government-issue. When he walked, his considerable weight rocked instantly onto his toes. The heels of his dusty, untied boots never disturbed the ground. His every move was jerky and quick.

He asked us in rapid grunts, motions, and incoherent words if we were going to Thunder 1, then he said, "Why the hell are you not on my truck so I can get out of here?" He motioned for us to put our gear in the back of his truck and then for us to climb in the truck and be quick about it. It was at this point I recognized the driver. He was Carl, the worthless kid who sat behind me in Miss Whitson's fifth-grade class.

Carl had disrupted the class so badly that I hated school, I hated fifth-grade, I hated Miss Whitson, but most of all, I hated Carl. He bounced like a wounded kangaroo but in an irregular pattern that was as maddening as the noise of his back thumping the desk he occupied. The writing surface of his desk banged the back of my desk for as much as five minutes at a time. His feet would bang my butt until my patience started to fail. I still have a small black scar on my right shoulder blade where he jabbed the sharpened end of his yellow number two pencil. He told Miss Whitson he had meant to use the eraser end.

Just days before I performed the major surgery I had been planning for Carl, he and his mother moved to a nearby town and took Carl to "a better school situation."

I was now at the mercy of a larger version of the fifth-grade tormentor I had so despised, and I knew that for as long as it took to get his truck down Highway 1 to Thunder 1, I had to be civil.

Out of fear, I took a quick inventory of the armament on that rolling dirt bag of a truck. I had been issued an M16 and two clips of ammunition, which I clutched tightly. Slim carried his knife. Carl's sole weapon was a 12-gauge shotgun. It was a Winchester model pump, my grandfather's favorite. Carl's shotgun had so much dirt on it that I am sure that, if it did fire a round, the pump mechanism would never move to allow a second shot. He had the thing tied with electrical tape to an improvised ring on the dashboard just in front of the shift mechanism. In even a minor shootout, we were in big trouble, and we could not count on Carl.

Carl's truck was a regular supply truck, and on this particular trip, he was delivering C-rations, mail, and ammo to Thunder 1 and two base camps farther north. Carl was obsessed with his mission. He was a delivery man, and he got the supplies to the correct base, to the correct drop point, at the correct time. He must have been late on this trip.

Highway 1 was a paved road dedicated to two lanes of traffic, one in each direction. The section we were traveling was flat and straight. There were no posted speed limit signs, but I am certain Carl exceeded the lawful limit. By the time we were in sight of the base camp, there were vehicles on the road ahead of us. By the halfway point, I was far more concerned about the possibility of a fatal truck wreck than damage from enemy activity.

As we approached the entry gate, it was obvious that the

guards knew Carl. As soon as we were in sight, they jumped behind the sand-bagged barriers on each side of the entry and yanked the barbed wire gates as far to the side as they could reach. Carl did not acknowledge the respect. He rammed his truck to the supply point and stopped without bothering to slow down. He had killed the big diesel engine before the wheels stopped rolling. He was out of the cab and in the bed, throwing cargo to the ground well before Slim or I could find the door handle, open the door, and slide out to the ground, and relative security, of front-line combat.

THUNDER 1

THE THUNDER 1 base camp was the size of a major college football stadium. The turf, however, was red dust. There were no above-ground structures. The camp was home to two 8-inch guns, three mortar squads, various artillery pieces I never learned by name, and a squad of 1st Infantrymen on standdown and pulling guard duty for the camp.

The few men we saw were moving slowly but with purpose. To a man, they wore steel pots covered with camouflage cloth and a veneer of red dust. The guys were without shirts and sported world-class suntans. A few had cut their pants off just above the knee for style or comfort. There was no trace of rank insignia, but it was obvious to even the casual observer which men were running the show.

Slim and I wandered around an hour or so, unable to find anybody willing to admit they were expecting us. We finally stumbled onto a staff sergeant who seemed to know the system. He was just returned from R&R and awaiting contact with his company. Sarge assured us someone would come for us. He invited us to hang out with him and told us to be patient. We had come upon Sarge as he was intently watching the flight of a projectile from one of the 8-inch guns. The gun operator assured us he could drop a round from that thing into a five-gallon bucket eight miles away. I was impressed but not convinced.

The 8-inch gun was mounted on a mobile bulldozer with a grader blade behind it. The blade was dropped into the dust before the gun fired and took most of the recoil. When that big boy did fire, it erupted with enough noise to wake the residents of a large cemetery. The kick pushed the gun's carriage backward three or four feet and drove the blade well into the ground. The dust from the concussion left everybody close to knee-deep in red dust.

The mortars were not as impressive, but we checked them out anyhow. The operators spent a lot of time setting the rectangle baseplate, calibrating or recalibrating the dials of the bipod, organizing the booster charge bags, and adding new sandbags to the low circular wall, which protected the weapon from incoming rounds. Each mortar had a crew of three men. One man was the squad leader. He did the important stuff and was the man who dropped the shell down the tube when all the calculations had been done. The other two men were called ammo-carriers. I am sure they must have done more than that. There was lots of activity there, but no rounds were fired all day.

Darkness set in. Sarge had found a foxhole position near a guard station, which offered a waist-high wall of sandbags for additional protection. We settled in for the night beside the guys assigned to that guard position. The men were in a deep discussion concerning the effects of pesticides on the world's food supply. Before we could weigh in with our considerable knowledge, a loud explosion occurred much too close to us.

As if no one had noticed, every voice on Thunder 1 roared, "INCOMING." Those screams were followed closely by a much softer but more urgent call of "medic."

Slim and I grabbed our packs and—in unison and with much too little regard for the potential danger to our persons—headed in the general direction of the plea for help. There were no more explosions, and we found the wounded men near a perimeter guard bunker. Two soldiers were awaiting our attention. One of the men had a two-inch cut on his right forearm, and the other was bleeding from his calf but had not yet removed his pants. I could not see the full extent of the wound.

Slim took the arm wound and applied a pressure bandage, which stopped the bleeding. He poured some hydrogen peroxide onto the wound site and wiped clean the area around it with a 4x4 gauze. He picked up a tongue depressor we used for application and spread an ample dose of the yellow antiseptic salve we carried and used for most everything. He covered the prepared wound with clean 4x4s, wrapped the whole package with white paper tape, and pronounced the man ready to return to combat.

I went to the man with the leg wound and, with my shiny, unused bandage scissors, cut off his pants leg at knee level. When I got the wound exposed, I found a shallow cut of maybe three inches, and the bleeding pretty much stopped. I applied a pressure bandage, which stopped the bleeding. I poured some hydrogen peroxide onto the wound site and wiped clean the area with a 4x4 gauze. I took a tongue depressor and spread an ample dollop of the yellow antiseptic salve. I covered the wound with 4x4 gauze, wrapped the wound with white paper tape, and pronounced the man ready for combat.

Mr Forearm Wound was wise to the ways of Army politics. He knew from our cleanness and general glow of innocence that this was likely our first experience with combat and the practice of combat medicine. The man did not ask about the care of his wound, did not question his fitness to return to duty, but he bluntly, or maybe threateningly, asked, "You guys do know how to get me my Purple Heart, don't you?"

There were many thoughts attacking me at the time, but the treatment logbook and related paperwork for this man's Purple Heart were not among them. Slim got the man's information. I did the same for Mr Leg Wound, and we retreated to our night position to digest surviving an enemy rocket attack and dealing with real honest-to-goodness war wounds barely a week into our combat assignment.

DREAM

IT WAS DARK when I got the paperwork complete on Mr Leg Wound—the kind of dark that made lighting bugs look like flying kerosene lanterns, but the dark cover lifted soon. Someone on Thunder 1 or our command headquarters decided we were in imminent danger.

Two "Huey" H1 helicopters suddenly appeared to the west of our position. Both choppers were equipped with spotlights like I had never seen. They began to systematically sweep those lights in the open area outside our perimeter wire and then away from the wire as far as the land was open. I watched with concern but saw nothing out of the ordinary.

One of the choppers turned off its light, and it looked to me like the light show, excitement, and entertainment were over for the night. But the pilots were not about to give it up. The grizzled trooper beside me said, "You ever seen a 'minigun' work out?" Before I could confess my ignorance, the chopper with a light still burning gave out the loudest fart from hell and rained continuous machine gun rounds into the open ground under its light. It continued to drench all the open ground around Thunder 1 with the same medicine.

My neighbor informed me the gun was a pintle-mounted M134 7.62mm minigun that could sweep a football field and put a round in every square inch of turf. I was instantly a true believer and in love with the thing. If there were unfriendlies when the gun kicked in, they were not there when it hit the whoa button. Word spread that we'd do a recon at first light and, for now, to consider the area secure and get some sleep.

Our small group made beds, arranged packs, and positioned weapons before going to sleep since we were not responsible for guard duty. Sometime later, but well before daybreak, the permanent recurring dream visited me for the first time.

In the dream, it is the two a.m. to three a.m. guard duty assignment. I am positioned in a foxhole with my M16 resting on a bank of sandbags, the weapon directed at the perimeter wire. In addition to the barbed and rolled wire, there is a chain link fence some five or six feet tall. One of the Viet Cong regulars, dressed in black pjs and carrying a satchel charge, walks cautiously toward me from somewhere dark beyond the fence. He climbs effortlessly to the top of the chain link. I can see the man as clearly as if he were an image on high-quality photographic paper. He looks intently side-to-side, hunting for the perfect place to leave his deadly explosive.

I have my weapon loaded, safety off, and know without a doubt that it is my responsibility and duty to kill the guy, but I cannot will my finger to operate the trigger mechanism. I cannot command any part of my body to move. In the brightness of that total darkness, the enemy and I make long and deep eye contact. I somehow know my next best option is to alert the other guard position. My scream sticks in my throat. I am totally paralyzed in fear and drenched in more sweat than the night temperature requires.

BANANA

I WAS NEVER much of a breakfast eater, but Sarge had stumbled upon a bunch of bananas he was gushing about, so I decided to try one. The fruit was a little over half the size of the bananas we regularly bought at the A&P at home. They were nearly green and kind of firm. I was not sold on them, but figured they were not likely to do me any permanent harm.

I hesitantly took the largest, yellowest of the remaining fruit in Sarge's collection and slowly peeled it. The pulpy meat inside looked no different than the A&P version, but once I tasted the thing, I had no doubt the A&P had been cheating me big time for a lot of years. The texture was cool, consistent, and firm without hardness. The taste was sweeter than the best sweet tea in Georgia.

I was trying to figure out how to relieve Sarge of the few heavenly bananas he had left when the squad leader from the nearest mortar unit walked up. Carl, the truck driver, had come in with the day's supplies and brought with him a platoon sergeant who was to take Slim and me to A Company. Still being new to the working of combat chain-of-communications, I asked the squad leader how he happened to be the one to bring us orders. In a matter-of-fact voice, he said, "The platoon sergeant off-loaded his gear at the bunker entrance where he met an ammo-bearer of number one 8-inch gun position. He told the ammo guy he needed the two new medics to meet him at the gate, ready to go to the bush ASAP. The ammo guy went back to his bunker and told his squad leader. His squad leader knew you were on the base, but he was not positive where. The squad leader found one of the mortar crew members who knew you were on the east side of the base somewhere, and after asking a couple other guys, he found out I knew you were here. You two better get your stuff together and report to the gate."

Slim did not have a pesky M16 to carry, and he was standing with pack secure and ready to move well before I struggled to my feet and became painfully aware of the weight I was being asked to tote. It occurred to me that some of this vital equipment might not be so vital.

We waddled to the gate in search of a platoon sergeant. The only GI at the gate other than the military-looking guards was a loud, not-so-tall, but quite round man with an overblown air of authority, which was not congruent with his outward appearance. The man's pants were at least a size too small, and too much of his pasty white butt glared at the world. The first two buttons of his shirt were either unbuttoned or missing and revealed a heavy crop of black curly chest hair. His boonie hat was crumpled and adorned with two The Big Red One patches attached at rakish angles. He had a dusty, untrimmed mustache and was in bad need of a bath and shave.

Platoon Sergeant looked us over quickly and was easily satisfied that we were the two newbie medics he was to pick up. He did not laugh at our cleanness and innocence, but I could feel him wanting to or doing so inside. I took a quick inventory of the equipment this leader had staged on the sand-bagged bunker of the guard post. His only weapon was a dirty M16 with a twenty-round clip of ammo fixed in the gun. I looked hopefully for additional ammo or grenades, but there were none. His backpack had been stripped down to the aluminum tube frame to which was securely strapped a couple cases of beer.

Then, moving like a factory worker hearing the bell at shift change, he swung the pack onto his shoulders, picked the M16 up with an experienced hand, and headed for the gate. I followed blindly, now impressed by the agility and natural strength of Platoon Sergeant. We moved quickly out of sight of the base camp and walked a narrow dirt road through an open forest of hardwoods. It could have been one of many places I had hunted rabbit with my father, but I knew that, even in his red Chevy 4x4 with oversized tires, he could not rescue me here.

LT

THE ROAD, AS we followed Platoon Sergeant into the jungle, was more of an oft-traveled path. It was smooth with a sand base and no trace of the red dust I had tramped at the Thunder 1 base camp. The path soon became a trail wide enough for two people to comfortably walk side-by-side, with edges worn level enough to allow groups from opposite directions to pass. There were no tracks or grooves to indicate the path had ever seen wheeled traffic and no hoof prints anywhere. There was no evidence of domestic life, but I was sure this surface had been exposed to its fair share of human activity.

We had not traveled ten minutes before we came to what I can only think of as a crossroads. It was a design layout the Georgia Department of Transportation could have planned and constructed with their best and newest instruments and equipment. It was perfectly square, and the roadway was straight as far in the distance as I could see. We marched straight ahead.

The trees around us were tall. I felt sure most would reach eighty feet into the air. They had straight trunks with rough bark and no limbs below forty feet. They were spaced forty-five to sixty feet, just enough disharmony to rule out the symmetry of a tree plantation. I tried to name the tree varieties. They looked to be oak, maple, and locust, all rolled together.

I am sure I could have followed a more scientific identification if my mind had not been occupied with the possibility of finding an enemy gunman behind each of those magnificent tree trunks. I knew it was beyond human capacity to climb the limbless trunks of those trees, but I found myself searching the lower branches for signs of the dreaded sniper.

The leaves of these great trees filtered the sun's rays and left a soft and consistent light under the forest canopy. Those same leaves, which were so efficient at deflecting the blinding light, were not so good with the heat. The offensive heat from that sun came right to the forest floor, and somehow, the leaf canopy held the overpowering heat at eye level.

Twenty minutes into this walk in the woods, I became painfully aware of the weight I was carrying. The pack frame was eating a hole in my back at a place I had adjusted incorrectly, and the sheer weight was turning my legs into wobbling noodles.

Platoon Sergeant was still churning at full steam. He had not stopped at the crossroads, and he did not look in either direction at the intersecting roads. If he paid any attention to the surrounding landscape or looked any direction except straight ahead, I did not see it.

Just before I knew I was going to drop to the ground and freeze up in a permanently cramped fetal position, Platoon Sergeant slowed down and began searching the roadside and underbrush. We moved at an intense snail's pace for thirty feet or so, and without ceremony, Platoon Sergeant raised his M16 high above his head and moved off the path to our left. It seemed logical to me that this was the place where we had found our company and Platoon Sergeant would listen to the guards give the challenge word and then give them back the correct password for the day. I heard no challenge and certainly no password, but after the salute of the high M16, Platoon Sergeant led us into the perimeter positions of A Company.

There were three guys huddled in the guard position we walked through, and, except for the man charged with watching for enemy advance, no one looked up from the card game in progress to see who was coming into camp or why. The instant we were out of sight of the guard position, Platoon Sergeant pointed the barrel of his M16 to our right and said, "LT is forty feet over there." "LT" was a new term to my military vocabulary but obviously a short

Troubled Sleep

form of Lieutenant and, in this case, Platoon Leader.

Slim and I looked in the direction Platoon Sergeant had pointed and saw nothing to indicate a military position. I turned back to see if Platoon Sergeant might be a little more specific. He had vanished off the face of the earth and left no evidence he had ever existed.

Slim thought he saw evidence of a path to LT's position and started moving. I was not going to face the jungle alone and was soon close behind him. We came on a group of seven or eight men eating lunch. Slim reported to LT, who asked our names and, without looking up again from his beans, told Slim he would need to report to the captain, but I was to stay.

LT sent the one guy who was finished eating to take Slim to meet the captain. He looked at me and said, "Sit down over there with John and Tom and eat. We'll be moving out in two hours."

I slumped in the direction LT had pointed, happy at the prospect of removing my pack, not at all pleased by the "moving out in two hours" comment.

Tom turned out to be the platoon machine gunner. Even though he was on the ground, it was obvious he was as tall as any man I had seen in military uniform. The bottoms of his pants stopped mid-calf. He wore long olive drab, but not necessarily military-issue, socks that covered the part of his legs that would have otherwise been exposed. He confirmed that he was, in fact, Tom and told me that I would be assigned to his squad. He made no effort to be social. There were three other men in his circle of warriors. One of them was the John mentioned by LT, but neither of the guys offered their names or any conversation.

There was a large tree close to Tom, and I leaned heavily against it and slid my backpack surface down until I was squatted firmly on the ground. Once sure the pack was not going to roll sideways and embarrass me even further, I slipped my arm free of the pack straps. Every muscle and bone from my upper neck to my butt screamed relief, and each individually swore to me they would never get back into the straps of that torture device. I sat in that awkward position until I was reasonably sure I could stand. Then, with less effort than I expected, I got up and stretched. I got back close to the ground and safety and grabbed the first C-ration can in my pack. I took the P-38 universal can open device from my side pocket, opened the can, and drank the contents.

The two-hour appointment to move out came and went. With the delay, some of my anxiety left also. In the space of an hour, I had become a member of a machine gun squad of a combat platoon. I did not feel especially welcome or wanted.

Without warning, LT blundered into our area and brusquely ordered, "Saddle up." I never heard that term in a military setting, but knew exactly what it meant. I went back into the full squat position, leaned against my pack and the tree, and, as gracefully as possible, inched my way back up the tree to a full standing position. To my surprise, a welcome surprise, I found the burden of the pack and its contents not nearly as heavy as it had been earlier in the day. I decided it would be good to see how the other squad members managed the "saddle up" routine, but by the time I was upright and in full position of my gear, the other squad members, except Tom, were moved to the assembly point. Because of the weight and awkwardness of the M60 machine gun he carried, Tom's "saddle up" routine was more complicated and time-consuming. He had his backpack in position before I was able to follow technique. He picked up the M60 by a shoulder strap attached to the weapon's stock and barrel. He placed the strap on his right shoulder and on top of the backpack strap. That left the M60 swinging with the trigger mechanism at the level of his right hand. There was a round chambered and a belt of ammo long enough to hang loosely across his left shoulder. Tom picked up a metal waterproof can of ammo in his left hand and was ready to move out. I had never lifted an M60 or a box of ammo for the weapon, but I knew very well the gear I carried was light by comparison.

We formed up in an open area and started into the woodland I had just come through to join them. The line of men was so long and spaced that I could not see the lead members. I did not hear the orders of movement, but the man walking in front of me and the man walking directly behind me were interested in only one thing. They watched every step I took and every bodily move I made. I pointed my M16 at an interesting plant and felt a sharp slap on my leg from the man in back of me. I looked too long at a crushed Pepsi can, and the man in front of me jammed the butt of his M16 in my stomach. I am no Einstein, but I quickly realized that I had better keep my full attention on the straight ahead. I could hear my mother telling me not to touch things as we walked the aisles of the local five-and-dime store.

I had no idea where we were going, why we were going there, who was deciding those things, or how we would know if we were there should we reach the destination. My mission was to be there in such a way that, unless someone needed me, no one would know I was there.

OHIO

MY FIRST COMBAT march ended before dark. We had found a trail which, to my eye, could have been made by animals. Using primitive grunts and gestures, LT placed the platoon in a loose circle, with the roadway roughly forming a midline. I was assigned to a rifle squad for the night and to the care of a young sergeant with a new mustache that showed little promise of maturing. He was 5'8" or so, and his features were perfectly balanced. The mustache was the only thing showing distortion. The man's eyes, nose, and mouth were in perfect symmetry with his classic oval head. His arms, legs, hands, and neck were all aligned, and the exact length, diameter, and form for his body. To me, the neatest thing about the man was that he was civil. He managed to keep his squad working efficiently and together without having to resort to language filled with anger, resentment, or fear.

The sergeant found an acceptable place for the squad to bed down for the night. The other members dropped their gear and prepared to do military stuff, to which I was not invited. They left me in the area of our little camp and told me essentially to be quiet and not touch anything until they returned. When they were out of sight, I moved my pack to an area as close as I thought comfortable to the area where the squad leader had dropped his gear. I moved it a few feet to a spot I thought might provide better protection to our heads in the event something dangerous happened. I took out my Case XXX knife with an eight-inch blade and dug in as deeply as I could.

My grandfather had always carried such a knife. When it came time for me to ship out, he slipped a new Case, like his favorite model, into my pocket. He had sharpened it to his exacting specification, which meant it was as sharp as metal could be. I have never

David Rozzell

liked to carry a sharp knife and carry a small scar or two to prove it. It did not take long before digging in the jungle dirt and removing tough limbs dulled the edge more to my liking.

I managed to get my sleeping quarters acceptable and was still waiting on the squad. The raw nerves supplied me with enough energy to fix a bed-down spot for the sergeant, and I took the chance that he would appreciate the effort rather than be upset at me.

The squad finally returned to the position where they had dumped me. They arranged themselves in a ragged circle of seven men. Each man was to sleep with his feet to the center of our circle and his head to the outside and behind a barrier of some kind as protection from enemy activity.

Earlier in the day, I heard one of the squad members refer to the platoon sergeant as a "Shake n' Bake." I was not sure if it was a term of endearment or if the man was being singled out as some sort of freak member of a military cult. When we were settled in for the night, and after he had given guard assignments, I asked him what the hell a "Shake n' Bake" was.

My ignorance amused the man, so he gave me the *Reader's Digest* version. The war in Vietnam was fought in small units in restricted terrain, so the noncoms who led many combat units alone were more important in many cases than the officers. Prior U.S. Wars had been fought in big, wide-open landscapes, and the fighting unit often had a general officer on the scene. There were not enough qualified NCOs to fill all the squad leader and platoon sergeant slots. He left unsaid the many casualties, which were a big reason for that fact. The Army, in its infinite wisdom, created an NCO school, basically along the lines of the already existing Officer Training School, to solve the problem. The program took the top-performing recruits from Basic Infantry Training and put them through twenty-one weeks of much harder schooling. At graduation, the candidate was promoted to the pay grade of E-5 and the rank of Buck Sergeant. It was, on paper, a good deal for the soldier who completed the schooling. The short side of the story was that the new Buck Sergeant could expect to be leading a rifle squad in the jungles of Vietnam within thirty days of graduation.

The "Shake n' Bake" came from the Kraft cooking product of the same name, which, in their iconic TV commercial, claimed to make baked chicken taste and look as "crispy and juicy" as the best fried homemade chicken. There were different sources credited with starting the name, which probably originated as a highly negative statement of the worth of these soldiers.

This "Shake n' Bake" may have been the exception. He was a mid-western all-American boy. He had been born and lived his entire life in a small town in Southern Ohio. He graduated in the upper tenth of his high school class, where he took a loving interest in making machines and doing useful things with metal. In his junior year, he won a third-place ribbon in the Ohio State High School competition for ornamental welding. His mother proudly displayed the gate and hinges he made as the entry to her Victory Garden.

After graduation, Ohio attended the local community college to study Tool and Dye Making, but after completing his first year, he fell victim to the draft.

I asked Ohio what we, as a unit of The Big Red One, were doing in terms of a military mission and why we were working in such small groups in the middle of such a large jungle. It was obvious he had not been invited to the latest Council of War meeting, but he knew what his squad was doing. We—I was a member now—were conducting search-and-destroy missions. Specifically, we were looking for the enemy supply routes of men, food, and weapons. We went out each night to trails believed to be traveled by the Viet Cong (VC) and set up ambushes to neutralize them.

So it turns out I was put out here—lord knows how many miles from home—in a jungle too big to measure, with six men I had never met before yesterday, carrying a small caliber rifle with "Made by Mattel" stamped plainly on the stock, camping on a trail of sorts, and waiting for an enemy of small soldiers to come marching along so I could blow them away. Made perfect sense.

David Rozzell

"Not to worry," Ohio said. We have a high-tech weapon we call a mechanical ambush device. Now, I felt safe.

Ohio went on to explain the contraption, and, as I feared, he explained it from an engineer's point of view. The business end of the gadget was four Claymore anti-personnel landmines daisy-chained together. I had no idea what a Claymore was, and I figured the daisy chain was some mechanism that made all the weapons fire at once.

He was carrying additional specimens of each part, so we slowed down, and I was given a little show-and-tell. The Claymore was a landmine with great destructive powers, a two-pound block of plastic explosive, C-4 in military terms. It was packed, in the front part of the device, with seven hundred or so steel ball projectiles. It was easy to tell which side was the front, as it had one-inch block letters reading FRONT TOWARD ENEMY. The shot spread out in a "killing field" to a fifty-yard distance straight ahead and a spread of thirty yards at that point. If aimed correctly, it had a one-hundred percent strike rate to the size of a man. The device was housed in a convex green plastic case, around twelve inches long, six inches high, and six inches thick. The overall weight of the unit was three-and-a-half pounds.

The explosives were set off by a toggle generator device called a "clacker," which looked like the spring device often used to strengthen the grip of old folks. The clacker generated enough electricity to touch off the blasting cap built into the Claymore. The daisy-chain effect happened when the electrical wire was attached in series so that the electrical current reached all the Claymores at the same time.

The process by which this weapon became mechanical was simple but not without possible complications. The landmine could be discharged with the current from a twelve-volt battery. Ohio carried a twelve-volt Eveready as a backup to the one he used to service the Claymores. He had a one-hundred foot roll of black electric wire like the wire used to attach lamps to floor outlets. He had stripped the ends bare of the insulating rubber coating and wrapped the bare copper wire tightly around the first jaw of a wooden clothespin. The pin was exactly like the one my mother used to hold clean, wet laundry on the metal wires in our backyard. To the other jaw of the clothespin, he attached a stripped wire of a shorter length—it must have been at least two and a half feet. He aligned the stripped and wound wire ends so that, when the pin was closed, the wires made solid contact, and electricity could run freely.

The equally expensive part of this machine was a white plastic spoon. The handle was inserted between the copper wire on the clothespin to keep the wires from touching and the electricity from flowing. When the spoon was removed, the current flowed through the wires attached to the battery—and at the other end to the blasting cap detonator—exploding the Claymore and killing whatever was to its front. The final step was to drill a hole in the business end of the spoon and attach a trip wire across the trail on which we expected the VC enemy to be traveling. When the unsuspecting bad guy walked by and hit the trip wire, his enemy activities ceased.

Before this discussion of high-level military tactics could go any further, my hour of guard duty came up. I moved to a position where I could better listen to the night noises and ponder the possible faults of this wonderful ambush machine.

CAPTAIN RED

THE NIGHT PASSED without incident. I even slept soundly for the few hours between my guard responsibilities. At first light, Ohio had the squad up, packed, and ready to move. We did not move, but we were ready. As soon as Ohio felt his squad was prepared, he took three riflemen with him to check the mechanical ambush.

Ohio left two men with me to protect the camp gear. I was grateful for the company. The men left with me were not particularly talkative. They noticed the sincere concern or outright fear in my voice, so they answered a few of the many questions I fired at them.

During the last of my guard watches, it occurred to me that we only placed the ambush protection in one direction of the trail we occupied. The trail went the other direction also. The smarter, if younger, of my friends assured me that the machine gun squad of our platoon was only a "click" down the trail and was protecting us from any activity in that direction.

How far is a "click?" Patiently, the youngster explained that a "click" was a metric measure of distance and a "click" was just over one-half mile. Why did we use the metric system? He had no idea.

The circular ground-sleeping position was designed to solve the problem of an enemy unit sneaking in from different directions. The VC our company and the other companies of The Big Red One had encountered in-country had traveled exclusively on paths. The leaders of the division believed it was safe to expect the VC would keep to their established habits.

The kid told me of the many booby traps the company had been victim of while operating in the area A Company had occupied for the last six months. The same VC enemy who was not smart enough to occasionally march off a beaten path knew the habits of many American boys of rural upbringing to kick cans, turn over funny-looking rocks, break dead limbs, and check out any bit of discarded trash. The industrious enemy had gotten good at placing grenades and other explosives under loose rock and Pepsi cans in such a way that when the can was moved, the explosive device detonated, and anyone close was severely injured. The youngster put his newly-introduced-to-shaving chin close to my face and said, "Never touch anything that looks out of place. Make sure nobody disturbs the strange."

Ohio returned while I was still digesting those orders. He clutched the elements of his mechanical ambush, which he had tightly wrapped and organized in the canvas pack he used to transport the device. He had contacted LT to get orders for the day's movement, and he and the men with him were in a buzz over the news of the morning. "Charlie" Company had suffered the loss of two riflemen during the night.

Each of my companions had an idea of what had happened, and each squarely blamed the red-headed captain of Company C. The speculations were that a squad had stumbled into a group of VC, that one squad had walked into the mechanical ambush of another, that the platoon had been drawn into a VC ambush, or that the sorry commanding officer had called artillery into one of his squad's positions. I got the idea. No one liked the Charlie Company commander.

The news fueled a lively discussion the rest of the morning. At 1400 hours, we were to join the platoon and hopefully get real news of the C Company affair.

At 1345 exactly, we saddled up for the one "click" march. I found myself taking my pack smoothly onto my back and accepting the march position of "man just in front of the rear guard." The man to my front stayed close to me and watched every step I took. He bumped me hard only once with his rifle butt, so I guessed I was doing better.

We met LT and the other squads with no apparent trouble. We were the last squad to report, but we were there at 1358, and no one seemed concerned about us. My fellow squad members filtered through the platoon, gathering news or gossip as we worked our way to our assigned outpost position.

Once we reassembled the story, the Charlie Company casualties took form. Captain Red, the CO of C Company, had a different operational procedure for posting guards and setting mechanical ambush devices. Red used the same equipment but felt his squad should not bed down for the night until the device was set and armed. He was afraid the enemy would see where his men had taken cover and then figure out where the Claymore had been set, find it, and turn it on his own men. If that was not the case, the clever VC could avoid the trail and trap he had set for them. He further believed that if he walked by his mechanical ambush, the enemy would follow him, thinking it was safe, and get caught by the tripwire.

The result in this case was he waited until it was so dark his men did not see their own tripwire and detonated the horrible device. He lost two men killed instantly and had two others moved by medevac helicopters to a field hospital where they were still alive and being treated.

Ohio got the squad gathered in the position. LT sent us down a bare slope with tall limbless trees, some one hundred and fifty feet away from the squad LT and his RTO were traveling with. The RTO was the man who carried the radio and shadowed the officer he was assigned to. We were not in sight of LT and his men but heard an occasional bit of rowdy conversation from them.

Ohio put two guys watching our exposed flank and demanded absolute silence. I had found the safest defensive position on the site, put my gear in a tight arrangement, and was working my way around the squad, hunting a few details on the C Company thing. Before I got the first question out, a skinny and dirty rifleman walked up to our position from the general direction of the LT position. The man stopped close to Ohio, looked firmly at me, and said, "Hey, you. LT wants to see you."

I picked up my rifle and followed the man to the ragged circle of men scattered around LT. I had not gotten a close look at LT when Slim and I joined the company. He was larger than I had thought. Overall, he was much larger than the average soldier I had seen. His skin was bleach white, and what of his hair that the local barber had not buzzed off was light blond. He wore military-issue glasses in a manner that said, "I'm a bully" rather than "I don't see too good without these." Behind the smudged lenses, he had sky-blue eyes which were intense but not especially intelligent.

LT did not stand, and without ceremony, he unbuttoned the fly of his pants and pushed them down to his knees. He pointed to the scarlet, blood-red, irritated blotch of skin that was his crotch. LT's mother had sent him a Gold Bond powder product that she assured him would cure his gall problem. The product had not solved the gall situation because it was not a gall problem. He had contracted a fungal disease of some kind. He looked at me and, with the voice he would have used to ask if I could change the flat tire on his pickup, said, "Can you fix it?"

I had a tube of topical antifungal medicine in my bag. I had no desire to see his rash at a closer distance, so I dashed back to my pack, found the tube, and rushed it back to LT.

When I got back to him, he had not moved but had thankfully reattached his pants. I tossed the tube in his direction. He caught the package with ease and even grace. He got the cap off and was applying the medicine before I could execute a complete retreat.

I returned to the squad to find Ohio fussing over his mechanical ambush device. He had wrapped the naked wires on the clothespin jaws and was checking the resistance to the spoon being pulled from its grip.

He went over the routine of setting the device and getting men set before arming the thing, and pointed out which men needed training and who could be trusted to set it up. The situation with C

Company really bothered him. He was adding an additional wire to the device to give him a way to manually detonate the unit if it was obvious there was a problem. He kept saying to me, or more likely to himself, "We shouldn't kill our own men."

Late that afternoon, Ohio was getting anxious. He personally inspected the weapon, ammo, and gear of each of us individually. Again. Just before he got on the last big nerve of the whole squad, he picked up his M16 and dashed off in the general direction of LT.

My squad positions got quiet at his departure. I pulled a notepad from the side pocket of my pants and started a letter. The youngster and his friend resumed a card game of some kind, and the guys in charge of security got serious about watching our flanks. The one member of the squad I had yet to hear speak got on his back with his head slightly elevated, pulled his boonie hat over his eyes, and went to sleep.

When Ohio returned, his mood was not improved. We were ordered to set up camp for the night right where we were. There was no logical place around our position to deploy a mechanical ambush, so we were to be a wing outpost to the squads who were deploying the devices.

Ohio ordered an additional man for each hour guard watch. Nobody liked that we were to get so much less sleep. When sleep positions were finalized, I took advantage of the time to experiment with different sleeping positions. The men I had been traveling with so far were tough and experienced in combat sleep. I was the sissy boy of the outfit. With experimentation and an element of pure luck, I discovered that if I leaned my pack against a tree trunk, stump, bank, or any bit of elevated ground, I could lay back into the frame and pack more comfortably than stretched out on the ground. Then, if I positioned the medical pack just right, it made a relatively soft pillow. It was not a La-Z-Boy, but in its way was a recliner.

At first light the next morning, Ohio and the squad took their rifles and all the ammo they could carry and joined LT on a recon mission. I was left with the young rifleman to protect our gear and position.

GOLF

I HAD HEARD one of the squad members call my young friend "Golf," so when he broke down his rifle and started his cleaning process, I asked if Golf was his name or his hobby. It was his name.

Golf had his M16 completely broken down with all the parts laid out on his poncho in textbook order. He was wiping the dust from each part with the cloth from his cleaning kit and then applying just the right amount of oil. He glanced at my rifle and reminded me how important regular cleaning was to the M16. He said, "A grain of sand in the wrong place can jam the thing."

I thought the man might know what he was talking about, so I found the cleaning cloths and oil I had been issued with the rifle. I was woefully aware of my ignorance concerning the weapon and figured I should get some training while things were quiet. I figured Pvt Golf would not try too hard to embarrass me. I had all the parts of the gun laid out as nearly as I could to the example Golf had set and was right proud I had gotten the thing apart and felt sure I could get it back together. The firing pin on the thing looked exactly like an aluminum 8-penny finishing nail from the revolving bin at the Ace hardware store I loved to visit. I was trying to feel how it might be different when, for the first time, I heard the unforgettable sound of an AK-47 rifle being fired.

The sound of enemy rifle was louder than the small arms I had fired and heard fired during training. It had a sharp, stinging pop to its report and screamed of sullen peril.

Golf was finished with his cleanup routine and had his weapon snapped together, a round of ammunition firmly chambered, and was in a defensive position facing the sound of gunfire before I could react. I had reassembled my gun and crouched beside the skinny kid before I noticed the shiny finish-nail firing pin was still firmly attached to the sweaty palm of my left hand.

The youngster beside me was alert and scanning the ground in the direction of the firefight. There was no panic in the kid, so I watched quietly with him til I had my wits about me, then attempted to put my rifle into working order. Golf told me that the action was a good two klicks away, so we were not likely to see any action from it, but I better get my gun assembled just in case.

Golf and I anxiously watched the territory leading up to our position for an hour or so. It seemed much longer. Then, in the filtered light of the late afternoon, a line of soldiers approached us from the general direction of the earlier gunfire. Golf knew immediately that the leader was Ohio, but he kept his weapon, with safety off, trained on the line of men behind Ohio until he was convinced the men were ours and that they were all accounted for. He charged me with watching the route to be sure no unfriendlies were following.

Golf went to the man he was closest to and, in an innocent way known only to the young, asked what had happened. His friend started to describe the event slowly and somberly. The other squad members did not seem to pay any attention and, to a man, were lost in a funk of some kind. Ohio walked quietly to his gear, sat down, and stared into the quiet jungle.

The story, as Golf heard it, found Ohio and his men in the second unit in line of march this morning. LT and his most experienced point man were leading down the trail that the point man thought showed recent human activity.

LT and his lead unit were concentrating on the straight ahead, but Ohio was more concerned with the area to the left, and he was the first to see the movement. A small group of VC was moving toward the path and had not noticed Ohio or the platoon. Ohio quietly put his men to the ground and behind trees. He signaled to the rest of the platoon to do the same.

One of the men from the squad LT traveled with dropped a clip of M1 ammo, and the VC opened fire on his position. Ohio killed two of them before the whole group of enemy realized they were heavily outnumbered and retreated. The rifle fire we heard after Ohio's first shots was triggered by relief, fear, or embarrassment by men who had hesitated. LT charged out to the killed when it was obvious the danger was passed. The ranking member of a unit of The Big Red One was charged with confirming any kill. LT did just that and took credit for the success. He called the CO immediately to claim the kill and ask permission to follow the blood trail he claimed to see and further engage the members of the VC unit who had escaped. The CO told him to clean up the area, return to camp, and prepare to stay in his current position for the night. With this information, Golf returned, still wide-eyed, to his sleep position, either grateful or jealous he was not involved in the shootout. Ohio got the guard rotation in place and collapsed into his night position.

For no reason I could think of I knew it was Monday. On Monday of each week, my job was to give a malaria pill to each man in my unit. This was my first Monday in charge of such an important task, so I took the bottle of hydroxychloroquine tablets from my medic bag and began to distribute the little pill to my men. The training film shows the friendly medic walking down a line of grateful soldiers who took the pill from the health provider and swallowed it with a smile. That is not what happened.

Even in his anxious condition, Ohio took his tablet and swallowed it without comment. Golf took his tablet from me but did not put it in his mouth. The other guys refused my offering outright. I protested as much as I was comfortable but was told in different ways, some not so pleasantly, "Those things give me the shits, and I can't do my jobs that way."

I took my medicine both figuratively and literally then walked off, hoping for better results next Monday.

When night settled in, I moved closer to Ohio and quietly started a conversation. I wanted to know what had really happened at the firefight, but more what had upset Ohio so much. He said he was not ready to talk about it. It was quiet for a short time, but he slowly told me it was different than when he went through training. The guys he killed this morning were not the hardened enemy murderers we screamed about in the hand-to-hand training sessions. Both the VC he killed were young and scared. The one who had opened fire on LT was wild-eyed with raw panic. His gunfire was aimed at ghosts.

Ohio knew neither he nor his squad were in the line of fire from the young VC shooting at them, but he had to protect his fellow platoon members. He saw his squad freeze as if watching a bad western TV show. The extra training Ohio had received took control of him, and he killed both VC with ease.

He was quiet again before saying, "It's not something to be proud of."

EAGLE FLIGHT

DAYBREAK FOUND LT at our campsite. He was proud enough of the previous day's operation to more than make up for the lack of pride Ohio found in the event. LT had talked with the captain before his visit with us. He knew the company was scheduled to move as a unit today and take a two-day standdown on a small firebase nearby.

The big boys at battalion headquarters had found an area several klicks away that the intelligence guys assured them was crawling with soft enemy targets. The proposal was a quick strike with one platoon in the hot area. The Charlie Company CO was well into his second tour and knew a few things about intelligence guys. He assured his commanding officer that his company had been in the field as long as The Big Red One expected for one mission and that they were in need of rest. Of course, with his experience, he knew they would expect more. Our CO vowed he would give each of his platoon leaders the opportunity to volunteer for the mission.

The proposal was to take twenty men into the area by helicopter, drop them there as a unit into the recon area, make contact with the bad guys they found, and kill the poor, unfortunate enemy. The mission was to end before darkness when the helicopters returned for them.

LT got wind of the deal and, with way too much haste and enthusiasm, volunteered his platoon, which, to my discomfort, was the platoon I was attached to.

Ohio took in the news without comment or visible reaction. Instead of sitting comfortably in a secure base camp for the next two days, he would lead a platoon back into the jungle. Ohio had now lost any innocence or illusions he may have cherished.

I was not a party to the mission plans, but the rumor called for a killing party, and I figured my services would not be required. When LT had finished issuing orders and otherwise spreading good cheer, he looked at me sharply and said, "Doc, get your gear. You will be traveling with me."

"Doc" was the universal Army name for any human connected in any way to the medical branch of the services. The name surprised me because it came from a man who had addressed me only as "Hey you" for the two weeks I had known him.

I followed LT back to his position. He gathered his platoon, except Ohio's squad, into a tight bunch and, with an excitement not shared by me or the other assembly members, started to explain the Eagle Flight mission we were given the honor of executing at daybreak.

LT had been an offensive lineman on the football team of a small mid-western college. I never heard how well he performed in that position, but there was no doubt he had the offensive part of the job title down pat. He jumped right into his pregame message. "We will load into four helicopters at 0730 hours. The choppers will take us to an area of enemy activity. We will have room for only six men in each chopper, so Ohio and his squad will not get to go with us. If things go well, we will get to do a similar mission with the whole platoon.

"Point and first squad will take the first two choppers. I will be in the third chopper with Radio and Doc. Machine gun squad will fill out the other spots.

"Leave all your gear here except weapons and all your ammo. Doc, leave everything here except your medic bag. Steel pot is mandatory during chopper ride and dismount."

LT did not open the floor for questions. I had many, but they were of a nature that I knew he could not answer. I kept my fears to myself and added my M16, ammo, and a pocketful of baseball grenades to the list of stuff I should carry. I found little comfort in the fact that I was to be on the chopper with LT. I had not met his RTO.

Even though all U.S. Army soldiers in the combat field of Southeast Asia during this time wore the same uniform and insignia, it was not hard to figure out that the man closest to the radio was in charge and that the square OD pack held medical supplies. Even with salutes and other symbols of rank forbidden so the enemy could not pick up the important targets, everyone knew that those close to the radio "bore watching."

§

At precisely 0800 the next morning, I was crouched with nineteen of my new friends in a secure landing zone (LZ), awaiting the arrival of four loud helicopters. To my surprise and delight, I found the RTO to be smarter than the average soldier. He had wanted to be a soldier, and as soon as he turned seventeen, he joined and asked to go to Vietnam. I was not a real fast learner, but I was seeing a pattern. The U.S. Army, for reasons known only to it and maybe God, took the request for assignment required of all inductees as a challenge. The few guys I had met in my brief stint as a soldier who had requested the war zone were sent to the humid beaches of Hawaii or the cold, snow-covered mountains of Germany instead. My RTO was a determined rascal and took his assignments to Panama and Ft Leonard Wood, Missouri, in stride and availed himself of a sound education in the ways of communication and the ways of the Army. He worked the system smoothly to get the assignment to Vietnam and, once there, had to make himself indispensable to the officers he carried a radio for.

My first conversation with RTO was interrupted by a low and screeching voice from his magic box. RTO handed the mic to LT, who grunted into the thing, then looked at RTO and asked the color of smoke for the morning, then grunted something into the mic. With that done, he screamed savagely, "Pop smoke." RTO had the red smoke grenade in his right hand and, at the command, jumped a few yards into the open LZ, pulled the pin of his grenade, and launched it mightily into the clearing. To my surprise, a large plume screamed out of a tin can and filled the field with thick red smoke. LT willed the group into the opening and prepared to mount the incoming choppers.

I attached myself to RTO and watched his every move while keeping a close eye on the mean-looking helicopters, which were rapidly dropping from a clear sky to the ground where I stood. Those flying buses, for all their speed and noise, touched the earth beside us with the grace of professional ballet dancers. RTO bolted toward the near side of the third chopper in line with LT, and I was in his wake. He hit the landing skid of the bird, turned as he was mounting, and landed softly in the middle of the open bay of the ship, his feet planted fifteen inches apart. He turned and helped LT up beside him, and, with great effort for both of us, he dragged me in and under the machine gunner.

I got my body and backpack stable, more in the frame of a sack of potatoes than a master military specialist, and my feet firmly planted in the basic fear-of-falling position. I had trouble finding a comfortable position for my rifle and banged the man operating the machine gun mounted just above my head. He shot me a look of vexation but not of surprise. It obviously was not his first trip to the jungle.

I grabbed all the exposed parts of the plane's interior, hunting for something substantial to hold. The back wall had a loose strap and a fold-down seat that I grasped with all my might, closed my eyes, and held on for what I figured was dear life. The big bird lifted even quicker than I'd guessed. When it leveled off, the ride felt smooth. I opened my eyes, shifted my weight some, and lost most of my fear of falling.

Once we were moving, it was not uncomfortable and the seats were like a family supper table. We flew around for a while, and I was enjoying the beauty of the massive forest. We were high above and looking down through the tree canopy I had spent the last few weeks looking up through. It was a magnificent sight. The trees were new-growth green with a tinted red-brown earth backing.

We flew high for ten minutes or so, then turned left toward a small blue stream. The covey of choppers buzzed the stream, then turned left again. The next feature I saw was a hard-traveled dirt road cut through the trees.

Our birds made a head-to-tail right turn and drop-to-treetop-level maneuver, during which my stomach scrambled to catch up. Once the group was over the cleared road, it dropped to twenty feet while still moving at top speed. There, the convoy slowed, and the machine gunners opened fire on the surprised trees lining the road.

I took a firm grip on the trigger mechanism of my M16 but could see nothing to shoot at. I became acutely aware of something hot hitting the exposed skin of my neck and back. I thought I had been hit. Quick examination showed no sign of bleeding. Closer examination and a more logical thought process proved that I was just getting pounded by the spent shell casing from the machine gun making so much noise at my left ear.

I had somewhat recovered from the machine gun scare when the helicopter's skids violently hit the roadbed. LT screamed, "Form up on me." He and RTO stepped gracefully to the ground and sprinted to the wood line. I knew enough to follow, but I stepped hard from the skid into a small hole and fell with all the grace of a wounded elephant.

My helmet jumped toward the tree line, and my body screamed and followed the helmet. I crawled for about ten feet, picked up my helmet, and checked my M16. By the time I got right-side-up, the choppers and my comrades were clear of the roadbed.

At the tree line, I found LT and the RTO busily getting the platoon lined up. I did another quick inspection and found that I still had all the necessary parts and was breathing normally. LT came to me last and said, "Nice dismount, Doc. Get in line behind Radio and try to keep up."

DUKE

THE NEXT OPERATION I was assigned to involved the entire company. The company's ranking medic was out of the country on R&R. Thus, due to the infinite wisdom of the Army at hand, the last in a string of chance decrees, coincidence, or luck, I was assigned to the company commander as his sidekick and personal medic. The significance of this position went beyond prestige and safety. The chance to travel beside Captain Duke was special.

The captain was a dead ringer for a young John Wayne. The captain was 6'4", and the charismatic leader John Wayne always played in the movies. Duke took good care of his troops and, while a stickler for detail, he was never mean-spirited.

The first day out was quiet enough. The captain was in a talking mood, and I enjoyed hearing him and having him alone to myself in quiet, small talk. This was Duke's second Vietnam tour. He admitted to being much seasoned since his first. What I remember most about that conversation was his philosophy toward the men in his charge.

Two years before, his first duty in combat was as a first lieutenant squad leader with the 4th Infantry. He had placed a squad of four men in a guard outpost while the company unit was breaking for lunch. The position was on a ridge point with visibility in every direction, and Duke felt good about the choice.

Duke was hit with a bad feeling about the men an hour later and went himself to check on his men. They had all been killed with so little resistance that neither he nor anyone in the main camp had heard a thing. He found poker cards from a game his men had been playing spread near them as if they had just gone to sleep and dropped the cards to the ground. As a commander, from that time on, he had been hard on card playing. The comment I remember most just before he said to me, "Go to sleep, Doc," came in a quiet, firm, compressed, and unyielding voice. It was, "When I got orders to come back here, I promised myself that I'd do my soldierly duty but that my personal mission would be to ensure that every man under my command would go home from here alive."

§

The next day was more eventful. Early afternoon, we got a call that a small group of VC had been seen a mile or so to our West. It was suggested we set up a base camp and send the three platoons to conduct a recon in that direction. We did so, and I settled into a position of safety as close to the captain as I could get while still protected behind a big tree stump.

The platoons left the slower members—machine gunners, medics, and slow guys—in a military position for which we put two-man guard posts in a circle some thirty-five feet from the center. The center was manned by the captain, his RTO, the artillery forward observer, and me.

The forward observer was an interesting character with no real purpose to this mission. The platoon and squad leader knew our position, called in artillery, and adjusted the accuracy after the first explosion. The observer was there to satisfy Army regulations, and he did carry a rifle. We were in some important discussion when the ammo-bearer of the machine gunner behind me approached quickly and quietly. I was not actively talking at the time, so he came to me and, in a frantic stage whisper, asked if there were any friendly Vietnamese units in our neighborhood. He and the machine gunner had just seen some uniformed natives walking not far from his position.

I stopped the officer's conversation and explained my thoughts on the gunners' situation. Duke got the radio operator to change frequencies so he could talk to the great guardians of military maneuvers about the situation. Too quickly, he was told to "take out" whatever unit was moving around us.

Duke looked to me a little too unconcerned that I was a medic, not a warrior kind of person, and said, "Doc, you go tell that machine gunner to stay where he is and do not fire on those people. Get back and let me know what is happening."

I picked up my M16 and casually walked to the position I'd seen the real soldier return to. I did have my helmet and the magazine of ammo in the weapon, but nothing more. When I got close enough to see the machine gun position, I was harshly waved to the ground and soon was aware of the reason.

Through a small break in the elephant grass to my left marched the whole NVA Army with assorted camp followers in tow. I informed the gunner and his ammo-bearer that Duke wanted them to keep down and not upset the bad guys. Then I took a close look at the party moving along single-file in front of us. They looked intent and were moving with purpose. I was sure I did not want to take them on.

Before I had finished my assessment of the military possibilities, the lieutenant of 3rd Platoon and his platoon came up behind me and demanded a report. I turned to him and launched into, "Captain says get down and stay quiet until this thing passes."

Somewhere between "Captain" and "says," the good lieutenant knelt down and saw what we were observing. A glare crept into his big blue eyes, his nose openings flared, and the M16 he was carrying came to life, firing in the general direction of the enemy.

I knew that my mission was compromised. I saw a frightened and angry machine gunner stand, put his M60 on his right hip, and send lead to join that of the lieutenant. I got caught up in the action and dropped onto the soft earth, pulled my helmet down, and started firing my rifle.

There was a lot of loud excitement for the next few seconds or minutes. I had, and have, no idea how long the engagement lasted. Things got quiet, and I saw the lieutenant and his platoon running in the direction of the departing enemy. I was aware that I had no ammo for my M16. I was ill-prepared to start a war and had no idea where the bullets I fired may have gone. The machine gunner was standing alone and wondering what the hell had just happened. I sprinted back to the captain's position as if I knew it was my duty to give him a situation report.

I found Duke flat on his back with a radio receiver in each hand. I have no idea where he found the second radio. He was talking to the general and alternately to the three platoons who were part of our little group. I explained to him the important issues of the incident as I saw them. The only thing he found important was that the 3rd Platoon was in hot pursuit of an enemy of unknown number and firepower. He absorbed things instantly, and I heard him click the receiver going to the command group and report to whatever general officer may have been listening, "We have engaged a large group of VC. We have put them in full retreat and are now in the process of following them and a few heavy blood trails. We'll find them no matter what it takes and destroy the lot of them."

The operations button had not completely closed before Duke had the button on the other radio on, and I heard him tell the ambitious 3rd Platoon leader, "Lieutenant, turn your men around and get back here to me NOW!" Duke called the other platoon leaders. They had seen nothing of an enemy. In a far calmer voice, he asked them to return to our position. After assuring himself that his outside children were safe and were coming home, Duke told me to go to the guard positions and make sure they were ok. I did get fresh ammo for my rifle and set off to check things.

The first position I went to contained my medic conscientious objector friend Slim. When I walked up on him, Slim was smoking one cigarette and holding a lit one in his free hand. He was traveling with the 2nd Platoon and was in this guard position with a soldier who was armed with a "thump gun." The thump gun, a grenade launcher that held and fired one grenade at a time, was accurate at twenty yards. Slim was in a heavy thicket and his handy pocketknife was not much protection. The position he was manning was ten feet from the path the enemy was walking, and Slim and his partner could only sit quietly and hope for the best.

With no verbal communication, Slim took my M16 and the extra ammo. He did not thank me. I watched, amazed, as he checked the weapon's mechanisms. He raised the thing into a firing position, seemed satisfied, and dismissed me. I never held that M16 again.

MONK

The men he led called him Monk.
He was smaller than most,
Not loud nor brash,
His glasses added a bookish look.
His energy level was high.

The platoon he led was slack.
Monk led them softly without fear.
"You might should clean that gun."
"Those cans need burying."
"That card game is a bit loud."
"That steel pot works better on top of your head."
"That opening's a good spot for an ambush."
"Let's not eat so loud."
"It's too quiet here. We aren't alone."

Monk saw everything, heard everything.
His men let him, stayed slack.
Monk too often walked point.
He reconned alone,
Set up ambush positions,
Armed the Claymore mine.
His M16 rifle was always clean.
It was rarely out of his hand,
Never out of his sight.
His followers were slack.

He had not been a monk.
After undergrad at Notre Dame,
He spent one year in Catholic Seminary.
He felt a different call, joined the Army,
Did the Officer Candidate School thing,
Joined the war effort.

David Rozzell

Monk loved his fractured country,
Was doing his part to glue it back.
His first field radio man heard he was Catholic,
Had studied to be a priest,
Dubbed him *Monk*.
It stuck.

When the day duties were done, we talked.
Is it wrong to kill the Viet Cong, Monk?
"There is a difference between murder,
And taking the life of sworn enemy."
Does your family support your mission?
"Sometimes.
I've learned a lot here about the human condition."
Does religious conviction help?
"I take care of my flock."
Does it bother you that your flock is slack?
"They have always come through under fire."
Is military discipline harder than the priesthood?
"Here, if I lose a member, it's permanent."
Is there a heaven and hell?
"We will all face a final judge alone."
Do you worry about dying here?
"If I do my job, I don't have time."
Are all humans sinners?
"All I've ever known."
Does formal confession help?
"The soul often needs relief."
Do you struggle with celibacy?
"Go to sleep, Doc."

HERC

SECOND LIEUTENANT MONK and his RTO spent more time than usual doing their morning planning and map work. I did not understand the magic of their work. I trusted them completely, but any time spent without posted guards and strong defensive positions bothered the place inside me tending to insecurity. The standard published procedure was to move quietly into a defensive position near dark and set hourly guards. This was known loosely as an ambush position. The other part of the protocol was to leave early morning before the bad guys got up and discovered where you were hiding. During the day, we traveled or stayed quietly in a strong, fortified place with hourly guards and waited til dark.

If Monk was worried about inactivity, it did not show. We were to join a machine gun squad from 2nd Platoon, and Monk wanted to be sure we were at the correct spot at the correct time with adequate wing security to bring the join-up off smoothly.

The join-up went well, and the day's march started. Monk did not walk point on this trek, something I was happy to see, but he was near the front of the line. I settled into the middle section of the group. There was no published information that said it was safest there and no protocol naming the mid-section as the position of the medic. I had started my combat career hiding in the soft mid-section. I had not been injured while traveling there and did not handle change well. The mid-section was my seat.

The couple of days that I had been humping with the 1st Platoon of Second Lt Monk, I had followed a young, quiet rifleman of unusual proportions. He had a round, pleasant, but not exactly simple face and the disposition of a well-trained draft horse. He carried more equipment than most. Rumor was he had been exposed to the use of explosives before being drafted. He had asked to carry the C-4 plastic explosives and the blasting cap on missions. Since the equipment was heavy, not to mention dangerous, and the company had no Army-trained explosive personnel, he got the job.

The thing that was distinctive about this man to my front was his body type. He was normal, even average, in the size of his legs and waist. His upper body told of a man who spent way too much time in a sweat-filled gym working out with a smart instructor of the Short-Armed Hercules Body Building Curriculum. The man was massive to excess in the chest and shoulders.

I was duly impressed by his physical presence, but the man was void of any emotion. I had been following him for two days and could not remember him saying a word. There was not a spark of anger in his eyes, and his actions were mechanical, deliberate, and, to me, just slow. On the march, of course, he had no problem keeping up. I noticed no evidence that he would do more than the threadbare essentials.

When the morning march started, the 2nd Platoon machine gunner and his ammo-bearing crew moved in behind me. I felt safer with the extra firepower so close. I knew it came with drawbacks, but, being simple, I held to the positive.

The machine gunner was a tall youngster—an athletic and engaging man. I liked him instantly. He stood just short of 6'6", a fact he mentioned often and always followed with, "A half inch taller and I'd ha' been too tall for the draft." As happens in the Army, he was called "Too Tall."

Too Tall would gladly share his story. He had been in his sophomore year at a small college in Western Iowa, playing basketball on a full scholarship, studying scholastically absolutely nothing, and preparing for a career doing the same. He was a handsome and virile fellow and popular with the female membership of the college and local community. His likable personality and lack of effort in the classroom turned on him, and he found himself at Fort Benning, GA, firing an M60 machine gun for the beginning of what should have been his junior year as starting all-conference power forward and college hero.

Forty minutes into the march, we heard the distinctive call of a rooster. To farm kids, there is nothing unusual or frightening about the high-pitched crow of a young rooster. We woke most mornings to the proud bird's innocent, if annoying, racket. In the jungle, during a time of war, for a military unit on a search-and-destroy mission, the call begets a different emotion.

The Viet Cong routinely kept a rooster tethered in their jungle camps. The reason behind the practice, as told to us search-and-destroys, varied. I heard they kept the beautiful male chicken we southern individuals called gamecocks around as watchdogs. They sounded the alarm when intruders were near. Another belief was that the enemy campers cooked them on weekends or that they kept the colorful animals as status symbols. The truth was we did not know why they kept them, but I do know that the shrill call sparked excitement and fear in my soul. The anxious among us worried at the size of the enemy group we were approaching. The aggressive locked and loaded their weapons and began to chomp on their bits ready to shoot it out with whatever size enemy showed up.

At the first piercing note from the rooster, my entire line of warriors froze at point like well-schooled bird dogs. Every eye darted and scanned the forest around us. By the time we were convinced there were no bad guys within the range of our guns, Monk was in the midst of us, as quiet as a summer breeze, directing everyone in a hushed whisper.

Monk said something to Too Tall, and the big man turned to his left and went to one knee while silently hefting the bulky machine gun he carried into a firing position. His skinny ammo-bearer got beside him, opened the metal box of belted machine gun shells he carried, and slipped the lead shell into position. The whole movement was as smooth and silent as a young fox running in freshly fallen snow.

Monk had the big man in front of me face to our right with his rifle and extra ammo close. He ordered the four riflemen behind the machine gun crew to drop their packs, pick up their M16s and extra ammo, and follow him to the rooster call. He charged me, of all people, to guard the dropped packs.

Monk led the group of attack soldiers off in the direction we had heard the dangerous call. I was amazed by the stealth, discipline, and purpose with which Monk and his crew moved away from us and then disappeared. I was also a little nervous about our defensive position.

We searched the woodlands to our front for any movement or hint of movement. Just as my anxiety level was decreasing, the sound of gunshots slapped us sharply around the ears. Initially, it was a choir of AK-47 and M16 music. It closed with nothing but M16.

Before my little group could get too anxious, a rangy figure with his M16 raised above his head appeared to our front and slowly moved toward us. Too Tall recognized the man as one of ours, and we relaxed and waited for news.

Monk and his stormtroopers had managed to surprise a small party of Viet Cong who were either guarding or digging a tunnel. The troopers had killed two of the enemy and run the remainder off into the jungle. Monk was awaiting orders. We were to stay put and guard the dropped gear. Monk wanted Herc to come up to the tunnel and bring the explosives.

When the word explosives was uttered, a major change hit Herc. His eyes bugged out and lit up like the Christmas tree on our courthouse lawn. He grabbed his pack and got the C-4 and blasting caps stuffed into the extra satchel he carried just for this purpose. Herc's movements became more like that of a herding dog than a mature elephant.

Herc and Monk's rifleman were barely out of sight when Monk walked up on us from the same path. He had decided, or been ordered, to set up an ambush position in the area of the tunnel he had just liberated. We packed up quietly and followed Monk to the new position.

The clearing we found was the size of a McDonald's parking lot. What made it unusual was the fresh red clay piled neatly near the center of the site. The soil was damp and appeared to have been dug out in the last couple of days. The tunnel looked more like the work of a big groundhog than the military construction of civilized humans.

I searched the clearing for a construction tool. There was no evidence of spade, shovel, or other grubbing instrument. Too Tall and I speculated for some time on what the tunnel may have housed or where it may lead. It was obvious that no human the size of Too Tall could operate in such an environment.

The question came up of the possibility of an enemy in the tunnel. The explosives were Monk's answer to solving that problem, but the company commander suggested that he hold off.

We started to settle in and prepare the area for our night occupation. There was a creepy feeling about the place, like if you ran an obnoxious neighbor out of his house and moved your cousin's family in for the night. It was hard to feel comfortable wondering if the neighbor you had just evicted had an angry, well-armed relative a few blocks away and planned to retake his house.

We set a perimeter and did recon to see from which direction we might expect company. Once we were reasonably satisfied, we tried to get comfortable. The surprised tunnel guards or diggers had left most of their supplies. There was nothing exciting, and it did not take long to inventory and discard. They had left two sleeping hammocks positioned between small trees. I had never been in a hammock and decided to see if they were at all comfortable. The units the enemy left were basic models, nothing more than nylon blankets with ropes tied at each end and then attached to the trees. I managed to get myself into one and found it surprisingly comfortable. I was entertaining the idea of sleeping there when I realized that I was suspended three feet off the ground, without solid protection from the bullets the local enemy might aim in that direction. With that image burning in my brain, I rolled slowly out of the swinging bed

David Rozzell

and crawled to a secure position behind a tree close to Monk, where I had left my backpack and rifle.

Just before dark, Monk decided that the correct solution to the tunnel situation was to blow the entrance of the ugly hole in on itself. He called Herc to the entrance for one last look.

Herc came to his side, clutching his bag of toys and moving as lightly as the lead ballerina in *The Nutcracker*. We watched him point to spots where he wanted to place charges and tell Monk how much damage we could expect and how the completed work of art would look. He told Monk how far the men in the audience would need to be away from the explosion.

Monk got us gathered up and to safety. We did not need much encouragement. From our safe position, we watched Herc dance and then, from his own safe spot, yell, "Fire In The Hole."

The resulting display was spectacular to the extreme, the mother of all overkill. The entrance to the tunnel was opened wide enough to form the banks of a respectable amusement park lake. It was deep enough to house the basement foundation of a North Georgia bank building. The noise or concussion of the blast left us all deaf and speechless.

When the dust fragments settled, we were able to see the evidence of the crime, and our hearing returned. I looked to see Too Tall and Monk standing frozen with a damp red clay coating on every square inch of their beings, except their eyes, which had broken the dirt when they opened them.

We looked in unison to the area where we had last seen Herc. He had gone to a kneeling position behind a low mound of dirt with a dead log on top. I thought at the time that he was much too close to the action. Now, where I had last seen Herc, there was damp red clay covering a form roughly the size of a human body. My medical training, to this point, had not prepared me to deal with a buried alive soldier. I panicked.

Monk and I bolted toward Herc at the same instant. We made less than two strides toward him before the clay mound that was Herc exploded, and the air was filled with a shrill squeal common to five-year-old girls when they find a talking doll with real hair and a frilly red dress under the Christmas tree. That outburst was followed by what can only be described as grossly inappropriate laughter.

We should have been relieved to find Herc alive and unharmed, but to a man, the platoon gave him the silent treatment for a couple of days. In the quiet that night, Monk assured me there would be no more explosive episodes as long as he was in charge.

YEARLING

AFTER A MONTH of traveling in eight-man units, being in a line of two full platoons was somehow comforting and somehow not. It was unusual not to have Monk walking point or close to it. We were near the middle of the long line, between Monk and our radio man, and we were heading for some map point where we would split up for the night and go back to our usual small ambush units.

The part of the march that was most troubling was a level stretch of unimproved road that seemed to go on for miles. It was bordered on our right by elephant grass and thick brush and on our left by an open field, which must have been pasture at some point.

It was late morning and hot and dusty. Monk was not talking. Radio Man was talking too much. We were going slower than usual, but I did not want to ask Monk what that might mean. I knew he had something working in that head of his.

I was just getting curious enough to disturb Monk when the brush and elephant grass to my right exploded. I knew instantly a squad of VC had seen us moving and waited until Monk and I, the soft underbelly of this beast, were in the right spot and launched an all-out assault. I found myself on one knee with my M16 aimed at the noise, and I had no idea how I got there. I pulled the trigger and got no response.

When the gun failed me, I looked quickly to the guys beside me. The noise got louder, and the eyes of my fellow grunts got bigger, but there was no gunfire. I relaxed my trigger finger but could not slow my heart rate nor explain why my gun did not fire.

Just when it felt like I would blow, a yearling deer exploded from the elephant grass. He dashed right beside me and nearly knocked Monk down.

The platoon let out a silent sigh of relief that could have been heard in Saigon. The deer crossed the open field, and when he got to the far side, every man in the group was laughing, a few rolling on the ground.

We humped the klick to the split-up point in silence. As we neared the point, Monk whispered to me, "Good job not firing into the brush at that deer." I had recovered some by then and, in a fit of honesty, said, "Monk, you know damn well I couldn't get this gun off safety."

BOB

In December, Bob Hope paid a call.
He brought a funny man, a drummer,
One golf club, a singer and a beautiful woman.
The tickets were cheap as dirt,
Liberty from jungle combat scarce.
It was Christmas. Was he our present?
He brought the fantasy of home to the fantasy of war.
The ticket holder in front of me gave me his.
Leaving my 10-man warrior band
To join a 1,000-man fun gang proved frightening.
The congregation in the jungle Temple stood out
Like a forgotten island in a Florida lake.
Our cargo chopper ride was rough and loud.
A road warrior near the front said too loudly:
"Nixon says we'll all be out of here by Easter."
The chariot kicked us out in a cloud of damp red dust.
The crowd cheered, laughed, cried, and clapped.
The event ended to a chorus
Of "How do I get home to my unit?"
The exit was as disorganized as a small herd of yearling deer
Surprised by the smell of a damp, mangy wolf.
I caught the last flight out.
It was as slow as Christmas.
Home with my squad, Monk greeted me with a knowing grin.
He quoted the Apostle John: "...now abideth faith, hope
and charity...,"
Then assured me: "here hope is probably the greatest."

OVER THE HILL

Over the ridge, through the thicket, over the hill,
Somewhere in front, sporadic AK-47 fire erupts.
The squad flattens.
Monk straightens, faces the report.
Over the ridge, through the thicket, over the hill,
An angry volley of M16 fire answers.
The squad questions, still flat.
Monk creeps to the ridge crest.
His radio found voice.
A second round of rifle music rolls,
Volume of the M16 and AK-47 now equal.
Over the ridge, through the thicket, over the hill,
B Company would love to have machine gun company.
Too Tall stands, shoulders his M60.
Tall's ammo man kneels, cradles his shell tin.
Monk scans the ground beyond the ridge.
Over the ridge, the squad chases Too Tall.
To the left, the thicket is thin.
Monk leads over the ridge into the thin thicket,
Through the thicket, over the hill.
Angry small arms talk again, urgently.
Monk leads Too Tall through the thicket.
The squad follows single file, anxious.
Monk stops where the thicket opens.
The squad stops. We all we crouch and check our sides.
The sound of battle stops.
The radio is quiet.
Monk hesitates, but continues.
Then a short burst of M16 fire shakes us.
Past the thicket, over the hill,
Monk dashes toward the hill.
Too Tall and his long legs stay on his heels.
At the top of the hill, Monk kneels.

David Rozzell

Too Tall swings his machine gun to his side.
They open fire together.
We move up beside them.
Over the hill, to our right, we see Bravo Company.
They have ceased fire, too spent to move.
Monk stops his fire and shuts down the machine gun.
Over the hill, we join B Company.
Confusion rules on order of battle and results.
As a larger unit, we return.
Over the hill, through the thicket, over the ridge.
Our night preparation complete, we talk.
Monk, did you know the bad guys would run?
"You never know what will happen."
How do you sleep after such a fight?
"I repeat my night prayer, turn right onto a sandy country road and sleep."
Monk, how do you know that road is safe?
"God paved it."
Don't think I will ever be that strong.
"Turn right and go to sleep, Doc."

WORD

Go inside *the word*.
Lt Monk spent years studying *The Word*.
"In the beginning was the word."
This morning, *the word* was "Monk, we're lost."
Our ragged line of warriors stopped.
The summer clothes of the jungle sheltered us from things civic.
Monk and Radio Man scattered maps and codes.
They wrangled over the lines and numbers.
Monk was *the word* and *the word* was "blue line."
Map blue lines are streets of water.
We saw no water, heard none, smelled none.
Monk said there was one. Monk was *the word*.
Our orders called for a meet with Company Commander at
1200 hrs.
1330 hrs. had passed in silence.
With compass and confidence in hand, Monk led,
A voice most literally in the wilderness.
We were directed by a clever novice,
At the edge a forgotten lawn of tender elephant grass shoots.
We beheld a pristine stream.
The group was surprised. Monk was still *the word*.
He ordered guard posts, set us down on the stream bank.
With a confidence we didn't share, he summoned The Commander.
Without assigning fault, he planned a join-up.
The Commander's soldier body was camped on the stream,
Its direction from our place no one knew.
Monk suggested they send up a red flare.
The Commander confirmed "a red flare."
We saw the glowing red flare.
The jungle and all who dwelt within saw the flare.
Monk ordered "saddle up" and led into the stream.
The water was as clear as freshly washed crystal.
The flow was bold, but not treacherous.

David Rozzell

It was as wide as a dirt road in the Alabama foothills.
The banks in places were over head-high.
Often the rocks of its floor were slick as black ice,
in places deep enough to the tender body parts above the thigh.
That was uncomfortable.
Thankfully we walked with the current.
Somewhere during the trek, the skinny kid carrying machine gun ammo snapped.
He dropped the heavy metal canister of bullets into deep water.
We all survived in good order.
Monk hand-pulled each of us onto dry land.
He reported to the Company Commander,
Spread our squad out with orders to eat.
Monk then motioned for the ammo boy to follow.
They disappeared silently back down the stream bed.
As we were burying the cans from our rations,
Monk and the penitent child returned.
The kid put the ammo near the gun and attacked his lunch.
Monk gently sat down beside me and prepared his meal.
To us, Monk was *the word.*

COBRA

MIDDAY, WE WALKED up on a group of VC frantically finishing the entrance to a tunnel. For some reason, the platoon moved in silence that morning. Our presence was a total surprise to the enemy construction crew.

Monk was walking point. I never learned to appreciate him doing that. He heard, smelled, or sensed they were ahead of us and got the platoon into a defensive position. My position at times like that was rear guard left side. I had it covered.

We were in high-canopy trees, old growth with a lot of distance between them. This gave the area the feel of a major basketball auditorium. When it was quiet, the feeling was not unlike that of a large cathedral. I tried to think of it more as a cathedral and hoped for the best.

Monk took the rifle crew to get a closer look and left me with Too Tall and his skinny ammo-bearer to guard the packs and his rear. He was out of sight when we heard the first shots. We could hear no voices, and Monk had Radio Man and his equipment. We were cut off.

It got quiet. I never liked quiet in that jungle. My little group saw every leaf that moved and tried to stay calm. Before I had much success, I felt the hairs on the back of my neck come to attention. I checked for enemy sneaking up on us and saw none. My eyes were drawn quickly behind and overhead of us.

There sat the meanest helicopter I had ever seen. It was quiet. How could something so big and powerful have hung motionless and silent? Where did it come from, and how long had it been there? My only logical thought was, *I sure am glad he is on my side.*

Before I could look around for any other activity, the bird released a rocket. It went right over our heads and took all the air out of the jungle. It turned another rocket loose, and with a smooth reverse twist, it was gone.

There was a massive explosion in the direction Monk and his boys had gone, and then a hush.

Monk and the rest of the platoon returned quickly. Too Tall and I pushed them for details without much success.

Radio Man finally summed things up. "I have heard that the VC is scared to death of the Cobra, but whoever named the machine came up short. It is far more a fire-breathing dragon from hell."

WATER

AFTER THE EXCITEMENT and stress of our slow walk, expecting to find gun-carrying bad guys behind every tree on the steep stream bank, our little group joined the company compound and a different set of anxieties. The most difficult part of a combat mission is inactivity. There is sound reason, if not pure science, behind the military fixation with drills, marches, police calls, inspections, sleep deprivation, and pedigreed harassment.

Our company was parked on the stream bank while the brain trust in Saigon decided where we were or where they wanted us to go. When it became obvious we were not to break camp immediately, Too Tall took his pen and letter composition pad from the plastic waterproof zip-lock bag in his side pants pocket and started a letter to one of his many lady friends.

The skinny kid who carried his ammo pulled a well-worn paperback book from his pack and climbed into never-never land. The rifle crew found a deck of cards and a smoke each and returned to a repeating card game.

I was leaning against a tree just short of a nap when Lt. Monk returned from a short council of war. He sat down and leaned into the tree next to mine. In our line of sight, roughly toward the headquarters group, were three Vietnamese soldiers.

They were dressed in camouflage fatigue uniforms, much like the Regular South Vietnamese Army soldiers, the ARVN, but the uniforms lacked emblems of any kind. There were three of the men in a tight group. Two of the men were in a squatting position the natives could assume for hours. We of the American South called the position "hunkering." I was never able to sustain the poise for more than two minutes. It seemed to me a poor substitute for an oak ladder-back chair. The other member of the trio was older, wiser, and a bit taller. He stood cane straight and rock solid between his partners and cradled an M16 in the crook of his right arm, a position I remember seeing Sitting Bull strike in a grainy photo advertisement for a Wild West show.

The guys looked like they thought they belonged with us. I was not as confident. Without taking my eyes off them but not otherwise pointing them out, I quietly said, "Monk, what's the deal with the local guys over there with the strange uniforms?" Monk did not look in their direction but said, "Those are our Kit Carson Scouts."

I had a passing knowledge of General Christopher Houston "Kit" Carson but had no idea The Big Red One employed natives as scouts and certainly not that they named them after Kit Carson. I asked for more information. Monk said, "Early on, the Marines found some Viet Cong members who discovered it was more comfortable to be part of the U.S. Military effort than live the hide-and-hope life in the jungle of South Vietnamese insurgents. The Marines put them to work finding bad guys in the local village suburbs."

"Can we trust them?"

"I doubt it, but the big guys think it has a positive effect on the local population. Probably think it looks good to the civilians back home."

"Do we care what the locals think?"

"There are a few members of our congregation who believe that the individual members of the local population are truly part of the greater human race and have souls, hearts, and even brains. I met one just last month.

"It hurts my human self that our team treats these people with such disdain, but my military self says it's helpful to have such a low regard for the people who are, after all, our enemy."

"And you—a rational, religion-oriented person—are okay with that?" I asked.

"Sometimes."

"Aren't the differences between things military and things religious, like the intense training, hard to reconcile?"

Monk said, "The training mechanics of each are similar. The military keeps the trainee occupied with physical fitness, drills, inspections, and instruction in weapons of war every hour of the day except for the few hours set aside for sleeping and eating. The religious orders keep students occupied with prayers, reading, and attending lectures and sermons, except for the few hours necessary to eat and sleep. The lesson plan of each admits that an idle mind is the devil's workshop. The tricky part is feeding the fertile mind a robust diet that expands the student's core to a mature member of the particular community."

"So, who is wise enough to prescribe the food? It still seems we are headed for conflict."

Monk's radio man appeared at a determined gait, and Monk followed him to the company commander's position.

The odd couple returned too soon.

Before I could ask, Monk replied, "The CO thinks our miscue this morning has landed us on someone's naughty list. We're to hump to the high ground north of us and set up an ambush position. Word is there was some enemy movement there, but the CO thinks it more likely we're on a punishment detail."

Monk told me to get our stuff together, then went to each member of his squad and explained the new mission.

When he got back to me, he had swung his pack onto his back. He said, "Saddle up," and led us away from the stream bed. We humped much farther than usual, and the heat and steep grade took the starch out of us.

When we found a piece of real estate Monk was happy with, he set a perimeter and assigned the guard rotation for the night.

The campsite was not in a spot any military person would have considered for an ambush position. There were no paths or potential paths—the undergrowth was dense, not even evidence of wild animal movements. We were either being punished or exiled.

David Rozzell

Near total dark, the skinny kid ammo-bearer crept over to me and said, "Doc, we ain't got no water, and I'm weak of thirst."

Monk and I checked our canteens and discovered we had failed to top off our water supply before leaving that beautiful stream.

Monk had everyone in the squad check out their water and found we were indeed in a bad place. We could not go back to the stream in the dark even if we could have gotten permission from the CO. We were firmly in the doghouse of High Command, and it was not the time to be confessing more incompetence.

Monk knew there was a resupply helicopter due tomorrow morning. He went to each member of our squad and patiently explained the whole dreadful situation. He took the canteens from each man and poured the water from each of them into the near-empty one of Too Tall. Then he explained the ration plan and left Too Tall to supervise the distribution.

Too Tall had a unique bedtime ritual. He did not like to sleep with his boots on. Too Tall borrowed a couple of new sandbags from the base camp we had most recently visited, so they were usually clean and dry. Then, before sleep time, he would remove his boots, pull the sandbags over his bare feet, and fasten the tie string above his pants. The rest of the squad and, in fact, all the men I served with in the field slept with their boots securely in place so that if we were asked to move before morning, applying foot gear was not an issue.

After finishing his supervision job with the water, Too Tall took his boots off as usual, but he noticed something resembling a small black worm attached to the tender part of his left foot just below the ankle. He was not bad to panic, but when he tried to remove the thing and could not, he got concerned and, in a stage whisper, yelled, "Doc, something the hell has me."

I had never seen a leech but had seen pictures and heard horror stories about them. Monk carried the flashlight with the red filter and, rather than trust me not to expose us to the enemy with the thing, he followed me to the position Too Tall held down.

It was instantly obvious we were dealing with the slimy,

blood-sucking animal. The treatment was simple—you expose the ugly little animal to heat, it releases his grip, and then you squish the varmint.

The skinny kid ammo-carrier had recently taken up smoking and volunteered to light up and then hold the hot tip of his Marlboro to the leech. It was against all protocol to smoke after dark, so the kid was much too excited. He lit up and applied the heat from the tip of his burning tobacco stick to the bug far longer than was necessary to accomplish his task and was obviously enjoying the process.

The military medical protocol in such cases called for an inspection of the feet of all men who had suffered similar contact. Monk and I went from man to man and checked each man's feet and lower legs and then each other's. No one except Too Tall had fallen prey to the enemy worm. I was much more comfortable, and from that time, he always kept his boots on. The dirty, malformed feet of the infantry are a nasty sight.

We settled in for the night and reset the guard rotation. I listened shamelessly as Monk reported to the company commander on the water situation. He did not dodge any part of the predicament nor attempt to shift blame. The CO was not sympathetic. He reminded Monk we were due a resupply chopper in the morning and ordered him to keep order til then.

In the twilight between our watch and our sleep, Monk rolled his head toward me and said, "Doc, do you have siblings?"

I confessed.

He said, "My older brother thinks I'm over here killing babies."

"What kind of work does this man do?" I asked.

"He's a professor at a Liberal Arts college in our neighborhood."

"What does he teach?"

"He teaches freshman-level stuff, English Composition mostly. It's not so much his education leanings that concern me. I think he didn't accept my leaving school and ending up here.

"He knows I'm not the baby-killer type, but he's not ready to support this particular war effort."

I asked, "What are your feelings about our involvement here?"

"Doc, I'd rather be doing something safer and less controversial, but I'm here, and I would appreciate a little more support from home.

"I wasn't at the top of my class academically. I was questioning my fitness for the priesthood. Uncle Sam made it obvious he thought I was fit for his Army, so I decided to make the most of the situation."

"But Monk, you did OCS. Priests are leaders," I said. "Don't hide your light under a basket."

"It's time for your watch, Doc."

At first light the next morning, Monk called the CO. Our resupply chopper was delayed. Monk got no pity concerning our water problem. The squad was complaining more than I thought necessary. Monk listened patiently til mid-morning then he called us all into a tight circle and produced a canteen from his backpack. He had gotten extra before we left the stream and now shared it. When it returned to Monk, it was all but empty. He put the container back in his pack and put the guys back to their station to await the resupply call.

Sometime in the afternoon, and before we faced a full mutiny, the CO called to say that our resupply ship was in the air. He gave the radio man the map coordinates to the pick-up point and the ETA. We did a saddle-up with more energy than a group of near-death men should have been able to muster and headed toward relief—water, fresh food, and maybe mail. We all drank too much water, filled every canteen, and sloshed off in a new direction.

Fifteen minutes into the march, the man walking point hit a frozen point that would have done any field champion bird dog proud. He did not have to turn or signal—we all knew the meaning of that cue. We all froze except for the darting eye movements beneath each steel helmet and increased heart rates.

Monk silently moved to the point man. We had stumbled upon a short convoy of enemy rice carriers. They were definitely enemy—a few even carried AK-47s—but to class them as a military threat was a stretch.

Monk called Too Tall and his man up and put them at the ready. Then he lined up the rest of the squad so we had a clear field of fire. He patiently waited until the tail end of the enemy train was directly in front of us. The last two men of the deployment were carrying only guns, so it was easy to see they were pure soldier and enemy. Monk instructed us to concentrate on the gun carriers and then gave the order to open fire.

The gun battle that followed may or may not have included return fire from our enemy. It was loud, and the excitement level was higher than any life event I had ever known. Thankfully, there was no call for a medic. The quiet that followed the shooting was deafening. The smell of gunpowder was so strong it may never have left me.

Monk and two of our more wild-eyed soldiers rushed to the path our bullets had just cleared of enemy. Their recon effort did not take long, and when they returned, we all sat anxiously watching for a counterattack.

The company commander called, wanting details. Monk calmly explained that we had walked up on a small group of the enemy carrying rice to their friends. We took out the armed members of the group and disrupted the rice-porting mission. We captured one bag of rice dropped by a wounded or frightened enemy and saw two blood trails, which we did not feel led to follow. All our men were fine. We were waiting for orders about a nighttime position.

The report to 1st Infantry headquarters went more like this: The squad tracked down a major well-armed resupply detachment of NVA and opened fire on them. The enemy killed outright was six and five-hundred pounds of rice was captured and is no longer in the possession of the enemy forces. The squad followed two blood trails until they ran dry.

The CO called back and ordered us to set up an ambush position for the night on the trail we had just cleared.

By the time we were settled, well before nightfall, Monk received a call from Division Headquarters. We were out of the doghouse.

The division boss asked Monk if there was anything we needed. With a straight face and his pulpit voice, Monk answered, "It's really hot and dry here and men would appreciate some fresh water." We enjoyed a short chuckle and went back to the work of securing our nighttime position. Ten minutes later, we saw a two-seat light observation helicopter overhead. The co-pilot was a full-bird colonel with a big smile on his face. The pilot found an opening not far from us, and we watched the colonel softly drop two, ten-gallon plastic containers of water to the ground. He turned to us, offered a snappy salute, and left.

I turned to Monk and tried without success to come up with some comment. He shook his head and said, "To whom much is given, much is expected."

FIREBASE RAISING

LATE AFTERNOON, MONK got us into a huddle and explained that he had just gotten word from headquarters that we were to join up with the whole company for a security mission. The artillery company had picked out a new hilltop in our area and needed us to pull guard duty while they set up a perimeter.

I tried to get more information from Monk during our nightly talk, but he knew as little as I did. I did learn that we were meeting Charlie Company early tomorrow morning and that, while he did not know the exact distance, it was not a short walk in the woods.

We broke camp early and humped a couple of hours to the meeting place. We waited several hours for transports. Word trickled in that we would be flying out in Chinook helicopters. The Chinook looks like a giant banana with spinning blades on each end. The rating of the plane was thirty-three combat-ready men. They sent us two helicopters. We filled them up. I did not count, and we did not crash.

We arrived at the firebase quickly. The choppers did not land—we just tumbled out the tailgate of those monsters into a mass of downed trees and red dirt. A few bulldozers were frantically pushing the tree stumps to the edge of what was to be a new home for an artillery company. The more the dozers worked the tree remains, the deeper the footing got, and the higher the red dust rose.

By late afternoon, the dozer guys had dug out crude foxhole spaces around what was to be the perimeter of the firebase, and we were assigned one of them to guard. Monk put me with three men I had never seen before. I was not comfortable but trusted him to have a reason for doing so. We talked for a while, and then the ranking member of our little group set the times for guard rotation.

My first hour of duty was 1 a.m., so I got to sleep early. Around twelve-thirty, I woke up. There was no one awake, much less on guard. I remembered which man I was to wake up after my duty ended but had no idea who was supposed to wake me.

I managed to control my temper. I got in a comfortable spot and watched until it was time to wake my replacement. I managed to calm down and sleep a little. At exactly 2 a.m. I woke like it was mid-day and I was late for an English Lit class. I completed the transfer-of-guard responsibility and struggled to get back to a troubled sleep. That routine continued the rest of the night, and for the rest of the time I was in the war zone. At home, during any times of stress, it continued to be a sleep pattern.

Mid-morning the next day, Monk came to my position and told me to gather my gear and saddle up. Our platoon was moving out to set up an ambush position for the night.

Once out of sight of the other men, Monk asked, "Did you sleep any last night?"

I said, "No, but the rest of the guys did."

He smiled lightly and said, "That's what I was afraid of."

CAT

JUST AFTER MIDNIGHT, the squad was awakened by the unmistakable sound of four Claymores detonating simultaneously one-hundred feet from us. The blast and smell meant that one of our mechanical ambush devices had been tripped. It also meant a long night without sleep.

The rifle squad closest to us heard a lot of movement after the explosion and decided there was a large body of enemy in the area. The squad leader, not long in-country, was more aggressive than Lt. Monk. He decided the situation needed artillery backup. The squad leader got permission to call in some rounds from the nearest firebase and quickly did so.

In his haste, or the heat of battle, the squad leader did not inform Monk of the artillery rounds headed our way. The first rounds went off in the top of the tall tree Monk and I had picked for sleeping quarters that night. Fortunately, that round only dropped leaves and limbs on us. Monk scrambled to his radio man and called headquarters to see what was happening. By the time he got headquarters to answer, we were taking heavy fire.

I could only hear one side of the conversation, but Monk was swinging some unpriestly words around, and the artillery rounds got redirected immediately. Monk came back to our post, and we waited for daylight.

As soon as there was enough light to safely leave our defenses, the more military men went out cautiously to recon. When he was sure things were safe, Monk called for me to meet him and confirm the action. The trip wire to the mechanical ambush had been activated by the lead member of the VC group and there were two dead enemy on the trail. There was at least one blood trail leaving the site. It was the first time I had seen the damage a Claymore could do. No medic could have helped those guys.

We returned to the campsite, and Monk got on the radio to report the night's activity and find out what was next. Monk was told to sit tight and stay alert.

The answer came late afternoon. The headquarters people thought there might be more enemy activity in the area, and we should move south about one-hundred feet on the same trail and prepare ambushes for the night. Staying in one place over two hours in the jungle was two hours too many. Monk would do as he was told. We set up and checked every direction an enemy might approach. We dug in and found solid trees to stay behind. Then we gathered up all the trash we had accumulated for a few days and buried it.

Just before total darkness, we heard the c-ration cans being moved around. No one jumped or scrambled, but all eyes turned to the trash area. Scratching around was the biggest, blackest cat I ever saw. We always had cats around the house when I was young, but this thing took all the good, graceful, strong, fearless qualities I ever saw and packed them into a body Superman would be proud of.

No one spoke. The cat decided we had left nothing worth his time, stretched in the most balletic maneuver, and walked away.

Just before we reached the part of our conversation that night when Monk says, "Shut up, Doc. You talk too much," Monk paused and said, "In the middle of such a horrible war, isn't it something that we see something as majestic as that cat?"

CHRISTMAS EVE

WE ALL KNEW IT was Christmas Eve. No one mentioned it. There was no resupply helicopter with mail due for a couple of days. There were no presents or cards.

The Chaplain held special services on base camps, but we were in the jungle, a short terminal trip from anywhere, and broken up into eight-man ambush teams for the night. We sat down in heavy brush to eat supper and wait for twilight so we could move safely into our ambush site.

The site we were assigned left me more than a little uneasy. Our leaders had found a newly cut road as wide as I-95 into Florida. There was no pavement and no tracks or prints to indicate recent heavy traffic, but the ghosts were around.

The soldier types placed our mechanical ambush devices and came back and armed the deadly things. We formed a tight circle with some new growth elephant grass—maybe eighteen inches tall—for concealment and protection. The anxiety surrounding this campsite pushed thoughts of my other family, gathered around a warm fireplace exchanging gifts, to a back burner.

It was a cloudless night, and there was enough moon to light up the area, so I got to sleep in good order. When my guard shift started at midnight, I got oriented, decided which direction was most likely to produce enemy activity, and settled into the routine of classifying and categorizing the night sounds and sights.

At 12:41 a.m., I heard the prop noise of a helicopter. It didn't take long to find the form of the lone chopper moving high and slow across the sky.

The helicopter was well past me when I heard the mission of the night. From a strong speaker on board the plane came music.

The first tune was "Silent Night." All the emotions I had stacked so high and deep on that burner fell heavily on the tin-foil-protected soft parts.

I am sure the officer in charge of the music mission had good intentions, and I hope the songs brought warmth to the other soldiers in the area, but I could have done without them.

CHRISTMAS MORNING

THE CAROLS FROM the midnight music box lingered painfully in my mind. They finally left. The tears seemed to hang on longer, but they, too, dried. When my vision and composure returned, I gently shook Monk to let him know it was his watch. Monk affectionately stroked his M16 and dismissed me.

When I woke Christmas morning, the squad was sharing more than the usual friendly banter. Monk looked at me and said, "That singing chopper get to you last night?"

I flashed a guilty grin. He said, "I would have shared it with you, but I was lost in my own music." We let the subject drop.

Too Tall was making rounds. His mother had sent him a dozen of her secret recipe oatmeal, peanut butter, buttermilk, and molasses cookies. His contribution to our Christmas atmosphere and celebration was to share a cookie with each of us.

Too Tall's skinny kid joined us. He had eaten half his cookie, savoring it a crumb at a time. The kid was as excited as a child on Christmas morning should be. "My mother always started Christmas with fried apple pies. We never got many presents. I sent them my last pay so, this year, Christmas should be better. Mother took us to church some, but Dad said it was a big waste of time.

"One summer," he said, "some friends of mine were going to Vacation Bible School at a church close by. I thought, 'Hey, that sounds a little easier than the gardening, tree trimming, and firewood splitting I was doing all day for my dad,' so I joined up. It didn't work out well. When I got home, Daddy made me do all the work I had missed and beat me good cause I wasn't doing enough.

"Christmas was always good, though," he continued. "There was always plenty to eat then."

Too Tall began, "I always loved Christmas. My family is Methodist, and that bunch makes a big deal of the whole season. We have several carol singers. There is always a Christmas play. I have been everything from the baby Jesus to the biggest, wisest Wiseman.

"Momma always said I was the star," he said. "The prettiest girls were always there. I'd have gone and been in that play even if they made me play the part of the jackass. As long as I believed in Santa Claus, there was a new basketball, baseball glove, or bat under the tree when I woke up. Since then, I've gotten mostly clothes.

"Do you think I went to church for the wrong reason, Monk?"

Monk reflected slightly. "I don't know that there is a wrong reason to attend church. As a place to pick up women, it might be questionable, but you should expect to find a better-quality woman."

The skinny kid asked, "Monk, why do people really go to church?"

Monk said, "There are as many reasons as there are people."

The kid asked, "So are we going to Hell for killing so many Gooks?"

"Are you worried about that, kid?"

"Nah, it couldn't be worse than living with my old man."

Radio Man came into our loose circle and sat down heavily. He had been following our conversation and joined without an invite. "Christmas 1959, I got a bicycle. It was not a new one but was in good shape.

"My dad traveled a lot," he said. "Never was one to spend time with me. You know, we were just not touchy-feely people. Dad took me out with that bike that morning. He held the seat and the handlebars and followed me around the yard and then the drive and street til I got the feel of riding the thing. Then he, little by little, turned loose of the handlebars and the seat til I was on my own. He stayed with me that way til I got real confident. Then he stayed and watched me ride around. I could swear he looked proud of me."

Then he looked at Too Tall and said, "Thanks for the cookies, Tall. My mother and sisters make chocolate chip and walnut cookies every Christmas. There were always enough there to get good and sick on. I usually did." He paused, then said, "That music last night was a good treat."

Monk asked which carol was his favorite.

"I like all of them. 'Silent Night' has always been my absolute favorite, though. Mom sang it to us the whole Christmas season. She could have been a famous singer, but for having to care for us kids. What did you do on Christmas, Monk?"

Things were quiet for a short time, and I was not sure Monk was going to answer. He finally said, "When my brother and I were young, Mom and Dad always took us to a Christmas Eve Midnight Mass. We would get back home to find Santa Claus had come. It seemed like a big deal, but looking back, I'm sure it was just a big deal to us."

"Christmas morning, we got up early," he said, "had a big breakfast and went to my mother's folks' house in the country. The men of the family would go into the cold, wet woods and hunt squirrel, while Granny and the women cooked. Then we would eat way too much of whatever the farm had produced an excess of that year, open a few presents, and go home."

Too Tall asked what present was his favorite.

Monk said, "My grandparents once gave me a year's subscription to the *Reader's Digest* Condensed Book Club."

The skinny kid remarked rather quickly, "The only book around our house was a Bible, but I never saw anybody read it."

The radio crackled, and our attention was glued to the incoming message. Monk took the mic and dryly asked for the day's marching orders. Some numbers and letters followed and, except for Radio Man and Monk, who were fluent in military radio, we waited in the dark, expecting bad news until Monk told us what to expect next.

"Get the Claymore in and police up the area," Monk finally said. "We're moving to a small firebase a few klicks south to do a guard detail."

The squad went to their duty station and quickly stripped the campsite. Monk and I carried less baggage and were ready to move immediately. I took advantage of the short wait to ask Monk if he was using his experience leading this squad as preparation for shepherding a religious congregation when he got home.

"Doc, you ask too many questions. I'm doing my best to make sure every member of this outfit gets home in one piece." He gave me a look I still do not fully understand and said, "That includes you."

THE NAVY

THE PART OF my youth that branded hard memories coincided with the polio epidemic of the 1950s. I remember vividly talking about standing water providing the breeding ground for the polio organism. My mother, with good intent and innocence, I'm sure, planted the seed of mortal fear in my small but fertile mind. I was sure that the liquid of any body of water from a puddle to the Atlantic Ocean sought, as its main purpose, to infect me with polio.

We lived in a rural area with no ready access to a river or lake, much less a swimming pool. I was not tempted to take up swimming and was never in the deep end of a swimming pool until briefly forced to do so to graduate from college. The Navy was never a consideration as an alternative to being drafted into the Army.

As The Big Red One was preparing to leave Vietnam, someone with a star or two on his shoulder pad decided to put a unit of Army with a Navy crew for a few days. The Navy had assault boats patrolling the river and ocean shores. The Army squad would serve as extra firepower during the day patrol and then be put on the shore in ambush positions for the night. The main mission was to watch the river for VC nighttime activity.

My fellow squad members for the mission were Monk, Radio Man, Too Tall and his skinny ammo-bearer, and Herc. We got on board without incident. The boat captain moved us around a while, then stopped in an open area of water and invited everyone to swim. I settled into my favorite spot near the left rear and watched.

An hour or so later, the captain called everybody back into the boat. He drove us around aimlessly until the edge of dark and asked

Monk to help him find a suitable ambush site. The captain and Monk agreed on a spot, then the captain put us ashore and promised to be back for us in the morning.

Monk personally set up our mechanical ambush device, and we ate supper as usual. We spread out for the night after deciding guard times and were good and quiet and asleep quickly. At the midnight guard change, we disturbed a nest of whatever passes in Vietnam for fire ants. The ground was moist, so we had put our ponchos on the ground, but the monster bugs sounded for all the world like they were eating right through them.

As we moved to higher ground, we heard the drone of the Vietnamese mosquito. The river marsh mosquito in Vietnam leaves whelps on any exposed human skin. We were all standing and scratching in unison.

Herc had taken a position on the highest ground near us. He had not even heard us cussing. We all got on the small piece of land Herc was guarding, and for the rest of the night, we slept with bodies tightly pressed to another squad member. It was not something to write home about.

Our boat captain arrived as promised, and as soon as we were in open water, Monk ordered him to stop for our swim. Soap came from somewhere, and the squadron was in the water treating bug bites. The wounds were so bad I found myself converted instantly to a swimmer.

SKIPPER

WE SPENT THREE days with the Navy boat. Every day, they picked us up in the morning, wandered around until mid-afternoon, and then stopped for a swim.

There was a five-man crew on the boat, plus the captain, and we did not get to learn the names of any of the guys. The crew worked hard. They kept all the guns oiled and the ammo positioned and ready to fire. The floors and benches were all scrubbed and clean. The crew members were clean-shaven every morning, and the conversation was straightforward, calm, and businesslike.

Monk had gotten close to the captain. We thought he may have gotten too close. Any time we were on the boat, Monk and the captain were talking. It is possible our squad was a bit jealous. I am sure I was.

During the day, our squad was left to our devices as to how to fill time. After the first day, we could tell there was little to no enemy activity on the banks we were patrolling.

Too Tall and the skinny kid had a card game going with the boat's rear machine gunner. Radio Man shared his knowledge of things radio with the Navy crew member who handled the radio on board. Herc watched the bank on the starboard side, and I pulled guard on the port side.

Monk and the captain talked about motors, navigation, steering, and boats. They were so into their conversations that we, as a squad, alternated between worrying about surprise attacks and wondering why the Army had even bothered to send us to such a forsaken and safe place.

We still took an afternoon swim. Monk and the captain did not slow their conversations or check on us. I tried to listen in on their talk to see what of military importance we were missing. All I could tell was that they were unconcerned about war.

The site for the night ambush seemed to be no more or less than the piece of ground the boat was headed for as twilight approached. Monk asked Herc to set and arm the mechanical ambush devices. He even let him pick the spots. I prepared the night's sleep position, but Monk was not talkative.

On the third day of the boating operation, the squad got anxious. As we were leaving the boat for the night, the skinny kid pulled me away from the other guys and said, "What the hell is wrong with Monk?"

When we got to the part that night when I talked too much, I mentioned to Monk that he had seemed a little preoccupied and distant. I did not get to the part where I asked what was wrong or said that the squad thought they may have done something really bad.

Monk simply said, "My grandfather was a Merchant Marine. I never heard him called anything except Skipper. I've always wanted to be called Skipper, but living deep in the Corn Belt, I never got to ride in a boat. This is as close to being a skipper as I've ever come, and it's been really fun."

Then, as usual, he said, "Go to sleep, Doc. You talk too much."

RETREAT

IN MID TO LATE March 1970, the rumors that The Big Red One was pulling out of the conflict in Vietnam were confirmed. I had been traveling for a few days with the entire platoon of Lt. Monk. The men who were slack in the hardest of times became more so.

After we set up mechanical ambush devices, Monk called us all together and explained that this would be our last night in the field as members of his platoon and as members of the 1st Infantry Division. He also confirmed that we were not going home with the commanding officer and his flags. We went about our business.

I had spent most of my time in the field beside Lt. Monk, and we often talked too freely. I was full of questions after hearing this was the end of my duty with The Big Red One. Monk did not have answers. We did the militarily necessary things and stayed in our own worlds.

The next morning, we broke down our ambush position, knowing we had only a klick to march through a no-fire zone to our base camp.

Monk walked point as he so often did. Near the end of the march, Monk came back to me and asked, "Doc, you want to walk point a while?" No, I did not want to walk point, even from the airport terminal to the big plane that would take us home, but Monk had a way of making things seem simple and even important. I said, "Sure."

Monk moved in behind me, and for what was the longest twenty minutes of my life, I led a platoon of combat veterans. Every nerve ending in my body burned. I saw every leaf move, heard every bird tweet, the sound of every footfall in the platoon. I could not only hear but taste my heartbeat.

When we finally caught sight of the camp entrance, Monk quietly moved beside me, patted me lightly on the back, and walked us into camp.

The walk into camp was uneventful. We were assigned to tents. Monk went off to the officer area and the rest of us into equally hot, dusty, and uncomfortable quarters. I wondered why I had not found out how much longer Monk had in-country. I did not know where he was likely to be reassigned. I did not even know his complete name. There were other things I wanted to know about the man, and I was disappointed I had not learned more than I had in the time I was traveling so close to him.

I made a short mental list of the most important things I wanted to ask him. I wanted his full name and home address. If things worked out and I made contact with the man, I would be satisfied.

Late that afternoon, I was cleaning my M16 so I could turn it in to supply. Monk was there ahead of me and had his weapon in the tub of cleaning fluid. I went to the other side of the tub he was working from and started breaking my weapon down.

We had been a few days on salt water, and I had not taken good care of it. It was frozen tight. I worked as gently as I could but, in the end, had to wait for the fluid to work the rust loose.

Talking to Monk was not hard. We rattled on about the good times we had shared and the good men we had been with. We touched gently on the future and wished each other well on our next assignment. The mechanisms of my M16 started moving, and I put all my effort and concentration into getting the thing freed up enough to turn over to supply. When I got it free and looked for Monk, he had gone to his next assignment.

TO THE CAV

IN FEBRUARY, THE Big Red One packed its duffel bag and went home. I was left in the war zone and shuffled off to a replacement company in Bien Hoa. For four days, I waited there for assignment to a new company. The rumor and wisdom floating around the compound was, "Anywhere is fine as long as you don't go to the 1st Cav. Man, they are getting half a company wiped out every day." The relocation papers I finally got started with "to C Company 15th Medical Battalion 1st Cavalry."

Brimming with confidence, I flew into the dust-soaked airstrip of the one-time French rubber tree plantation near the Cambodian Border called Quan Loi. Still looking for good omens and positive thoughts, I pitched my duffel bag on the back of the jeep my new company had sent to fetch me. As I was stretching my leg into the passenger seat, a Chinook helicopter like the one I had arrived on, but fixed with a cargo net every bit as large as the chopper itself, screamed over my head. Something did not look right about the plane. Half into the jeep, I watched dumbstruck as the overgrown banana ship jumped upward as much as forward into the cloudless sky and broke savagely into two equal pieces no more than two-hundred yards outside the base camp security fence.

Six crew members were left dead in its wake. I got to the new company area during the chaotic search for these casualties but was aware only of the high activity. When I reported to the company headquarters, I found one bit of positive news. The company clerk was a fellow I had been close to during medic training in Texas. He was alone in the office and gave me a quick lesson on the day-to-day working of the company. In its infinite wisdom, the U.S. Army sent a set number of men to each such medical company. This number was set in Washington DC and the men who went to the medical companies were trained in Texas and given the job skill I.D. number of medical aid men. That number was 91A or some advanced variety of it. The medical company needed people to do things other than treat the wounded. They had a motor pool, cooks, clerical staff, radio operators, supervisors, and ward medics at a minimum. All these other jobs had Army job I.D. numbers, but in the case of the Army medical companies in Vietnam, the company was allowed to assign jobs to the men who showed up on their doorstep according to "the needs of the Army."

In the company I had been shipped to, the company clerk, my buddy, was responsible for sorting all this out. To show off his power, this clerk, my friend, asked me what job I wanted in the company, and just like I had good sense, I quickly said, "I want to do surgery and medical stuff." Then, just as quickly, this clerk made a few marks on an official piece of paper, and I was placed. He asked me if I had a driver's license. I had no idea the Army even issued driver's licenses and told him so. He pulled a pad of forms from a drawer in his neat-as-a-pin desk, wrote a few words, and handed me the document. Seems part of the job included driving the jeep and now I was legal.

With the important aspects of my new home and assignment complete, my friend and clerk personally took me to my sleeping bunker, showed me the shower and latrine, and accompanied me to the mess hall, where the afternoon meal was in progress.

Once the eating was polished off, I was escorted to the facility, which was to be my work duty assignment. When we finally got to the treatment bunker, the physicians and high-level medical staff had completed the routine work for the day.

The company commander was standing in the shade bunker holding court with an enlisted man concerning the Japanese political culture prior to WWII, or that was as near to the meat of the conference as I understood it. My clerk waited for a break in the conversation and introduced me. The CO was a tall, thin, and unsubstantial person from Kansas. His hair had the wave, color, and consistency of corn silk a week before harvest. He wore a clean uniform with the appropriate officer insignia, but his bearing was less military and more cloistered nun. There was nothing about him that suggested he would be able to administer an antibiotic shot for fear it might cause the patient undue pain. While knee-deep in a profession dedicated and proud of its down-and-dirty image, this man was so clean it hurt. I took an instant liking to the man.

We had talked for a few minutes when a mud-caked jeep charged up to us. There was a lifeless body of an equally mud-caked soldier slumped in the passenger seat of the jeep. My clerk friend and the clean-shirted man talking with the CO suddenly remembered important business they had to attend. They bolted.

The CO quickly found a litter, and we took the wounded into the treatment room. The commander doctor took a quick look and asked me if I had ever performed a chest tube procedure. My blank look was answer enough. He briefly explained that the man, bleeding in his chest cavity, had collapsed his lung. The surgical procedure was simply to cut a small hole in the chest cavity and insert a medical-grade water hose into the chest cavity to empty the blood and let the lung reinflate. Emboldened with ignorance, I agreed to perform. The CO looked at me and said, "I'll talk you through it."

The necessary tools appeared from somewhere, and, calling upon what little sterile technique I had been exposed to, I started. For no logical reason, I thought this was just what every lowly combat medic did when they were moved out of field duty. With no break in the job since the jeep arrived, I found myself cutting a 3-inch hole in the man's rib cage where my doctor had indicated, with the intention of inserting the tube my new doctor friend was holding.

Once the skin was breached, I was told to take the pair of blunt scissors handed to me and aggressively work them through the intercostal muscles between the ribs. At this point, things failed to go according to plan. When I entered the chest cavity, I was greeted with more blood than I had seen total in my life. It was warm, dark with occasional pockets of bubbles, bright red, and all-over sticky. I was so surprised or unprepared for the outcome that I stood frozen while my legs and feet were soaked by the discharge. The operation stopped and became a teaching opportunity. The young soldier had been beyond repair, and the operation I performed was more of a test to see if I had the nervous system to do this work all day, every day. For a second or two, the motor pool assignment looked inviting.

Before I had much time to reconsider, I was informed gently that "no military job is complete until all the paperwork is in order." I was introduced to the DD forms from Graves Registration, which declare to the immediate world that another good man is no longer with us. The service man's serial number satisfies all the major questions. The matter of 'cause of death' and 'signature of attending physician' affixed to the Army paperwork closes the book, chapter, and verse, of a promising life. I initialed and attached the TD tag that follows the remains of our dead friends. Then, I helped the doctor gently lift the mortal remains into a black plastic-coated bag and zip the bag securely. The doctor and I carried the package to the twelve-by-twelve outbuilding, which served as the company morgue, completing a process with which I was to become much too familiar.

PURPLE

THE VILLAGE REGULATORY agency ruling the breeding of dogs around our base made no effort to limit breeders to pedigreed animals. The local Parrot's Beak dogs resembled the dogs at home only in that they had four legs and teeth, barked, and were always hungry and fertile.

The soldiers in Charlie Company each adopted one of these animals, and they were usually given free access to the company area. The situation reached maximum capacity, and an officer with too much time on his hands decided we had to cut out the dogs.

One of my roommates, who had just brought home a freshly weaned pup, was not going to accept the situation. He pushed me into the company jeep, and we went to see the Cav JAG officer. To my surprise, we were able to walk right into the office of the captain and chief lawyer on base, who also had too much time on his hands.

The JAG man proudly displayed his Harvard Law School diploma behind his desk. He had as high an opinion of himself as you would have expected and looked down a long aristocratic nose at us during the whole meeting. For no reason I could grasp, I liked the guy.

After thumbing through a few books, he informed us that U.S. Army regulations allowed for one and only one mascot per company, and we should consider cutting our numbers.

We thanked the man and left. After that, I ran into him a time or two on base, and we talked briefly. He was good enough not to ask me if the dog situation had changed.

A couple of weeks after meeting the JAG lawman, we had a late afternoon rocket attack that hit close to our treatment facility. We were real busy for an hour or so, treating the wounds of the few guys who were close to the explosion. No one was killed, and all the wounded were sent back to duty. I got settled into my night routine, hoping for a full night's sleep.

When things got quiet, I noticed a figure in flip-flops, cut-off fatigues, a sleeveless sweatshirt, and an oversized boonie hat sneaking into the facility. It was my favorite Harvard lawyer.

He had gone out in the dark to relieve himself. He had done his business and headed back to his bunk when the rocket exploded not far from him. He panicked, stepped off the gravel path, and cut his foot on something sharp.

He was embarrassed and had sneaked into the aid station when he saw I was alone, expecting me to fix him up and not spread the word to the whole base. It was not a real cut, but I made it seem as bad as I dared and then got out the DD Form for "medical treatment and disposition." He protested, saying he would rather this did not get on his permanent record. I assured him it was routine and that I would take care of him.

The next morning, I reviewed the incident with my CO and top MD. The good doctor was as far from Harvard and aristocracy as can be. He looked the treatment report over and asked a few questions. Then asked me point blank if this individual was the JAG officer. I told him it was.

He asked me why I had not recommended the man get a Purple Heart. I was caught. I said simply that it was the responsibility of a Medical Office to do so. He let that one slide and let me worry about the issue for a few minutes. Then I added that I thought the man would rather not have the medal under such conditions.

The doctor asked, "Was there an enemy attack at the time of this incident?"

I said, "Yes, sir."

He said, "Was this man in the vicinity of the explosion?"

I said, "Yes, sir."

He said, "Can you say beyond any doubt that his wound was unrelated in some way?"

I said, "No, sir."

He calmly signed the authorization for a Purple Heart and said, "Let the Ivy League S.O.B. Hero explain this to his grandkids over Thanksgiving supper."

JAKE

THANKS TO THE nimbleness and speed of the U.S. Helicopters, the 15th Medical Battalion attached to the 7th Cavalry of the United States of America was able to dispense medical aid over a large area with only a small group of men. The base camps our individual companies worked from did not need large plane landing strips or large roads for trucks. The mobility of our helicopters meant critically wounded men could reach large, well-equipped hospitals, leaving less need for personnel at the first responder triage treatment stations.

These same factors meant we did not have enough men to field softball, football, soccer, or even basketball teams to compete with other companies in our battalion. Fifteenth Med did, however, supply a competitive outlet. That competition was the "Soldier of the Month" contest, which decided, on the first Tuesday of each month, which company could present the sharpest overall enlisted man as determined by a panel of independent officers.

I had been a member of Charlie Company 15th Med, laboring innocently as a medical aid man for three months when my friend, the company clerk, marched into the back of the treatment room where I was attacking the middle of some tedious novel and announced that I was to be the next 15th Med Soldier of the Month. Until that speech, I was blissfully ignorant of such a title. I was not invited to try out for the engagement, and it was brutally obvious I was expected to win.

The next day, after my sick call duties were completed, a clean-cut soldier found me. This man was clerk of our small ward, and, as small as our company was, I had never seen him. He drug me to the mess hall and we started my training.

The first rule of Company C and Soldier of the Month was straightforward. "Top has never lost the Battalion Soldier of the Month contest, and it would not be healthy for you to break the string." He informed me that we had only three weeks to get me ready for the match, so every afternoon after mess call, someone would be assigned to educate me on a specific part of the test. It never occurred to me to question why me, or whether I had any say in the matter, or even if maybe a promotion in rank might follow a successful completion. There was also the worry that if I should finish second, a Court Martial might be in my future. The pressure was overwhelming, and I was overwhelmed.

The first few days of instruction were easy enough. One of the advanced-level medical aid men reviewed emergency medical procedures we used every day. I felt pretty confident about my knowledge of this subject. Of course, I had no idea what the test questions might be, and part of the test would concern military presentation and protocol.

The military knowledge part of my instruction was given by the Executive Officer, the XO, of Company C, Captain Sharpe. I knew him as the dimwit who often hung out in the treatment room where there was no work to disrupt him and sought free medical advice about his many phantom medical ailments.

I discovered quickly that the XO knew the military nitpick. Our first exercise started with him measuring twenty-five feet on the floor of our treatment room. He marked the ends of that measurement with two-inch-wide white bandage tape. He made me march the distance between the tape marks until I could take exactly ten steps and finish with the toe of my boot stopped firmly on the next line of tape. Once I could manage that task with some consistency, he began to work on my form. My arms were too loose, my knees had too much bend in them, I was not landing with enough weight on my heels between strides, I made too much noise at impact, my head was inclined too far forward and tended to move too much, and my shoulders were slouched. I was starting to question how I ever managed to walk to the latrine before his assistance. I worked on the walk problems every step I took from then until the test.

Once the XO saw me improving on the march, he started worrying about the stop, start, and the about-face. The halt had to be soft, sharp, and quiet, and it had to hit the tape mark at exactly the right point.

Then came the salute and report. The salute must start at the halt and be a continuous motion to the point one inch above the right eyebrow. The report voice had to be a precise decibel and in a tone that was understood by people from the South as well as those from the North of our great nation. The salute and report had to be executed with strong eye contact to the receiving officer. Then, eye contact was broken, and the down motion of the salute began exactly when the officer in charge returned the salute and acknowledged the report. The officer required an at ease. When asked, I was required to perform a snappy parade rest position and await further directions. This part of the performance was not as cut-and-dried as the other maneuvers because each charge officer had his own timetable as to when a new part of the routine should start and finish, and to anticipate orders was a major fault.

Knowing how to perform these tricks was one thing, knowing which officer to report to another. My slug-turned-drill sergeant assured me he would take care of those details. I obeyed the man, but I did not yet trust him.

As soon as my daily sessions with Captain Sharpe ended, one of the medical technicians was waiting with a few more pages of questions about sterile technique or CPR or some equally fatiguing medical problem. This was more comfortable until the addition of military protocol was tacked on. For some reason, the chain of command was important. I learned and somehow remembered the basic positions and, largely because I wondered if he was a relative somehow, remembered that a Gen. Thomas was the surgeon general in Vietnam.

Just after dark one afternoon, when I had enjoyed about all the military education I could stand, a mud-caked Army two-ton truck stopped in front of our office. Three men, as mud-caked as their truck, climbed down and walked into the admitting office. The largest man was holding something I guessed was a pup. We had gotten something of a reputation for being a place to bring injured pets after business hours.

The man was carrying an animal, but it was not a dog. It was a small monkey. I had seen a few monkeys on base and had run across families of a hundred or so in the jungle. The soldier called them "Howler" monkeys. They lived high in the trees and moved with the speed of light, but they managed to make sure you knew they were there. This, however, was the first time I had ever touched one in my life.

The engineer told me the story of the monkey's illness and that the animal's name was Jake. Jake had been with the company of engineers for eight months and had never been in poor health. He had free rein of the company area and, except for a habit of occasionally stealing food, was a model citizen. This morning, one of the men was preparing to blow up a small rock outcropping to clear the bed of a road and had unwrapped a new stick of C-4 explosive. Jake saw the man working with the explosive material, which is a plastic bar wrapped in cellophane, not unlike the wrapping of a good sandwich, and must have considered it food. Before the soldier could stop him, Jake grabbed a crumb of the volatile material and swallowed it. As the day went on, Jake got sicker, and the company more worried. I told them this was not something I had ever seen, but if they would leave Jake with me, we'd do what we could for him.

After a little hesitation, Jake came to me, and the engineers left. I listened to his heart. The rate was fast, but the rhythm was good. His lungs were clear, and breathing did not seem labored. I checked his temperature and recorded it. He weighed in at nine pounds. I would like to have known his blood pressure, but the machinery we used on humans was much too big for this animal. I knew, even as I performed it, the exam was an exercise to comfort my feelings of inadequacy.

Armed with what hard medical facts I had, I called the doctors' quarters. Our company CO answered. He listened without comment to my problem. He matter-of-factly told me that he was not sure what we could do for the animal this long after the ingestion of the explosive. Then, without hanging up the phone, he talked to the other doctors. He came back quickly and said the only treatment they could agree on was sedation of the animal and see if the body could process the stuff on its own. He recommended 0.5 cc of valium in a muscle, preferably the thigh.

The prospect of a monkey bite did not excite me, but I figured Jake was so weak I'd be okay. I got the med in his thigh muscle without incident. Jake soon got less responsive, and I was certain I had killed him. I found some wool blankets, formed them into a bed, and put Jake softly into the warm cradle. My real job at the time was to man the emergency treatment room, keep the meds organized, the place clean and supplied with bandages, and have things ready if we had casualties flown in during the night. The treatment facility after hours also served as an entertainment facility for MPs, truck drivers, pilots flying night missions, clerks, common soldiers wanting free medical advice, and others inclined to be awake late. Most nights, when the socializing stopped, it was quiet, and I read or slept on one of the litters we used to offload medevac ship.

This night, I moved Jake and his makeshift bed so I could see him if I woke up worried or if he should wake me. Before I found sleep, I noticed Jake seemed restless. I had been around dogs and cats since birth, and it seemed natural enough to place the little patient by my side. I covered us both and went immediately into a warm, peaceful sleep.

When I woke up to check and prepare the treatment area for sick call, Jake raised his head and moved around a little. I reported to the company commander, who agreed we had done all we knew to do for Jake and suggested that getting him back to familiar surroundings was probably the best plan.

The aide clerk found the engineers, and they came to the office to pick up their mascot. They were as mud-caked early morning as they had been the night before. I told the group's leader what we had done for his pet. He was concerned about long-term problems. I told him that we did not know what the future would hold for his monkey, but our honest opinion was he best enjoy every day they had with Jake.

Jake seemed happy to be back with his family. The muddy second-in-command engineer took Jake onto his shoulder and carried him toward the truck. Jake gave me one quick, noncommittal glance and went back to war.

I had nine days of training remaining before the competition. I had been introduced to, and drilled hard in, all the elements of the contest and figured I would now be in for some review and some downtime. Top had other ideas.

§

For the next week, every schooling session started with a full dress rehearsal. I was set at a door and marched to a tape mark twenty-six inches from a desk manned by my XO who pointed out every flaw in my march cadence, posture, and bearing. Then, we reviewed my report. Once that was sufficiently gnawed, the test questions started. If Top, the XO, and the surprise instructor of the day were happy, I was given a list of elements they thought needed review and improvement before tomorrow's session.

Before the start of lessons on the third day before competition, the fragile, lumpy medic who served as charge nurse to our company ward showed up in my office with a metal bowl of warm sudsy water and a sterile pack of instruments. He sat me at a table, spread out his tools, and sat down across from me. The medic put my fingers from the knuckle down into the warm liquid and let them soak. Then, with the softest hands I had ever touched, he patiently worked six months of dirt from under my fingernails. With surgical precision, he trimmed my ragged nails so that exactly one-sixth of an inch of finger was exposed in front of each masterfully curved nail. He dried each fingertip and admired his work. That done, he took a nail file to each nail to make certain that the curvature was perfect and there were no rough edges.

I was not comfortable through most of this operation. Holding hands with a male child was not something I was going to write home about. Mr Soft was unconcerned about anything other than his finished product. When he was satisfied, he wrapped his tools in the sterile wrap, poured the water from his bowl out the side door, put the wrapped instruments into the bowl, and, as he was preparing to leave, handed me two neatly hand-printed pages of instructions concerning nail care. He wished me luck and assured me that Top would have the procedure repeated if he was not happy with the finished product.

I filed the instructions and was back in my comfort zone when my buddy, the company clerk, walked in. Mr Clerk was carrying a right-out-of-the-box uniform. The shirt had my name over the pocket, the 1st Cav patch on the left arm sleeve, The Big Red One patch on the right sleeve, and my rank insignia on the tips of the collars. He had me put the shirt on and then made some corrections using safety pins. He had me put the pants on. He seemed happy with the way the pants fit, but before he gave me my old pants back, he checked my boots. He made some notes without comment, so I figured we were good to go. We talked a while about the course of the war. He was worried about an armed invasion of Cambodia. I assured him he had too much time on his hands.

It was dark and quiet when the clerk left. I quickly finished the work I thought would not wait til morning and started preparing my bed.

Before I got settled, I heard a baritone voice I knew I should have recognized. The speaker was an excited, if not scared, man and said, "I need to see Doc. He's done it again."

I walked to the office door and was met by the mud-caked leader of the engineering company and his small, hairy traveling companion.

Unlike our previous meeting, this time Jake made deep and direct eye contact with me, saying, in no uncertain terms, "I am scared. Please fix me." He left the engineer, plastered himself to my side, and pressed his head into my rib cage.

The engineer said Jake had opened an ammo box the company had been using to secure the plastic explosive and eaten another flake. The engineer did not think the amount was as large as before, but Jake showed the same symptoms.

I told the engineer to check back in the morning. We would do all we could. He assured me that Jake was back to normal twenty-four hours after I had treated him before, and he knew I would be able to fix him. No pressure there.

I called the medical doctors' quarters and told the CO we had had a repeat of the "monkey-eating-explosives" incident. I asked his permission to administer the Valium. My doctor friend agreed but told me to "lay down the law" to Jake's keeper. He never wanted to hear about the monkey getting C-4 again.

I got Jake medicated and let him sleep the night on my side. He was quiet and warm. The morning started earlier and was more frantic than usual, but then it became boring and routine. We had just medicated the last VD case of the morning when the mud-caked engineer appeared.

I took the man to a quiet place just back of the treatment facility and did my best to convince him to watch Jake more closely. He promised to do so, and I thought I had done my duty by the CO. I went to my little office and picked up Jake. He held my shirt, and we went to deliver him to his keeper.

I handed Jake to the engineer as gently as I could. Jake moved to his shoulder, and he walked toward the door. Jake sat proudly upright and turned toward me. We shared the strongest eye contact I had ever known. I could feel gratitude, admiration, and affection.

I think he even believed I was responsible for healing him. I stood mid-door, unable to break the eye contact, unwilling to return to my workstation once he was out of sight.

§

I knew a haircut was in my future, so I rather aimlessly wandered to the barbershop. I explained to the barber that I was to be involved in the Battalion Soldier of the Month game in a couple of days and needed to be clipped accordingly. He was familiar with the battle, and I left his chair nearly bald.

The morning of the competition arrived sunny, dusty, and hot. I was up early to get ahead of Top. He was up and arranging our equipment neatly in the medevac helicopter we were to take to headquarters company and the big show. The XO showed up right on time. We left the company area as it was waking up.

We were at the scene of the competition an hour or so before the other teams showed. On the way to the headquarters company area, Top marched me into a barber shop manned by one scary-looking Vietnamese local wielding a set of barber clippers older than dirt. I got another haircut, this time under the critical eye of my first sergeant. There was no one waiting for service, so Top left me in the chair and drilled me for ten minutes on the medical questions he was confident would come up in the grilling.

We walked to the office arena, where the XO showed me the near-invisible pencil marks he had made to serve as my start and stop marks when I entered the playing field. Then Top announced it was time to dress out. In a back room Top had claimed as his office, he had my uniform ready. My clerk buddy had altered them perfectly and then taken them to a starch factory. They were pressed so tight and stiff that I was afraid I would not be able to move. They softened up just enough. Then Top removed a pair of boots from a box that had no dust on it. The boots must have been patent leather. The shine and fit were far too perfect to have been military-issue.

Top got me dressed and stood up for his personal inspection, which included a look at my fingernails. He marched me to the headquarters company day room and the competition.

When my time came, I found the mark on the floor and stopped exactly on the mark in front of the head examining officer. The questions all seemed to have been lifted from the study sheets Top had walked me through a few minutes before.

To my amazement, I won the competition. Top patted me on the back and rushed me to the dressing room, where he personally repackaged the pretty boots and hung the uniform under plastic. I never saw them again. The XO came by and passed a couple of soft compliments. Then he and Top left me to find my way back to the helicopter while they visited with company bigwigs.

We got back to our company area just before the afternoon mess call. Top and I walked into the mess hall to cheers, but it did not take long for me to realize that Top was the star of this show and I just his latest work.

JOHNNY

AFTER THE PRESSURE of training for the Soldier of the Month contest and winning the event for Company C and Top, I was ready to get back to the softer routine of my medic duties. For whatever reason, the Viet Cong was not pressing the war as strongly in our area of operation, and that was fine with me.

I had been three days without three instructors demanding difficult things from me when my buddy, our company clerk, caught me leaving the mess hall after the evening meal. After the usual small talk, he informed me that the Soldier of the Month award carried with it a reward. I mentally started spending the extra $35 a month a promotion would bring me, but that was not what the Army and the 1st Cav had in mind.

In addition to the prestige of being Battalion Soldier of the Month, I was a day in-company with a colonel of the 1st Cavalry Division Combat Support Section as he executed his duties. And, as if one day of light duty was not enough, there would be another day set up to follow the commander of 15th Medical Battalion.

My clerk noticed my excitement and assured me it would be an experience I would never forget. That did not help. When I pressed him for more detail, it was obvious he had no clue. When I asked when this fabulous event would take place, he was better prepared.

"In the morning at 0800 hours, you will be at the headquarters office dressed in full jungle fatigue uniform with rank insignia on jacket and baseball cap." Then he said, "Lt. Col. Sams will have a jeep there to pick you up. Please don't do anything stupid. Top does not take well to being embarrassed."

As any soldier will, I presented myself for inspection and final orders from Top at 0745 the next morning. The portly First sergeant said, "Follow the colonel one full stride behind and one arm length to his right. Say absolutely nothing to the man unless he asks you a direct question, and then say as little as possible."

At 0800 hours, a clean jeep pulled into the front lot of headquarters. The colonel I was expecting had stayed in his helicopter, and I was met by a clean-cut, well-turned-out buck sergeant from the 7th Cav Headquarters Company near the airstrip. Buck and I had a short conversation on the short drive.

Buck had not spent any time with Colonel Sams but knew enough about him to prepare me a little for the excursion ahead. The colonel was an all-business kind of man and, on his good days, a certified asshole. I tried to remind myself that this was a reward.

The only thing Buck did know about our day was that there was to be a ceremony at 1st Cav Headquarters to install a new general officer. General Shultz, in charge of supply or something, was rotating back to the States. The colonel, with me in hand, was to attend the review and party at noon.

My driver dumped me much too quickly in front of the helicopter with the big yellow insignia of the mighty and war-ready 1st Cavalry. The engine was warm, and the blades already turning. The pilot had cleared for takeoff and acted impatient to be in the air. The colonel I was to shadow was strapped firmly in the co-pilot seat, impatiently shuffling important papers.

I had expected, with no sound reason to do so, that a colonel of importance would move about with at least an aide. The prospect of being alone with this hard-baked asshole bothered me far worse than facing down the Soldier of the Month Board.

Colonel Sams inspected me with cold eyes, glancing over Army-issue flight sunglasses. He checked off the nameplate to be sure I was the maggot he was expecting and, satisfied, gestured for me to sit on the bench behind him. The pilot pointed to the helmet on my left and pointed to my head to indicate I should put the thing on. I had ridden in a few helicopters but never worn a helmet. The thing was neat. It blocked most of the unmuffled engine noise, and I could hear the pilot and colonel talking, as well as the conversations they were having with the outside world.

The pilot took us very high, very quickly. I followed orders and said nothing. I did notice two things immediately. One, that my ears popped, and two, that it was cold. The scenery below was beautiful, fresh, and, if it had been defaced by civilization, had long since made a complete recovery. I had seen similar forest from the ground, but from the air, it seemed boundless. We had traveled for 45 minutes watching this woodland when I saw what must have been our destination.

On the highest mound of the area was a clearing that looked out of place. It reminded me of the bald spot on the head of an ancient monk, except the pictures of those monks always presented a perfectly round hairless area with precise margins, and the exposed baldness was always clean and without blemish.

The firebase we approached had been blasted and bulldozed in a violent fit. The surface was gaped and pocked. The perimeter was basically round, but at various spots lay large piles of logs and tree remnants in various stages of decay. The nude surface of the mound had earth-moving machinery and war-waging equipment parked totally at random.

Men were moving about, and even from the height of our helicopter, we could see a lack of military organization and protocol. None of this was lost on my colonel. The man started screaming and cussing so loud I wondered that they did not hear him. Not to worry. Colonel Hard Ass got his radio headset in touch with the commander of the base. There were a few technical military terms I didn't understand, but the curse words and browbeating were universal language.

We landed on the least groomed and dustiest spot on the base. The colonel jumped from the chopper the instant it touched dirt. He had his helmet off, colonel hat on, and command voice blasting before his jungle boots hit the soil. I was happy to be squirreled firmly in the back seat of the helicopter. I did not even consider following.

Colonel Blaster was back to the helicopter too soon. His face was much too red, and blistering curse words flowed until the helicopter was high up and out of sight of the offending firebase. I am sure we flew over some beautiful pristine country again, but I did not notice. I did see another firebase below and briefly wondered what I might do to warn the guys working it. I also hoped that the men on the firebase we just left didn't call ahead and instruct this bunch to shoot our helicopter down.

For reasons not given me, we passed over the next firebase, and another one. I guess not even the colonel could maintain such an intense level of anger forever.

We arrived at headquarters at lunchtime. The colonel pointed in the general direction of the enlisted mess hall. He told me to report to the parade ground after lunch and then went off to do colonel things.

I found the mess with a little help and ate a delightful serving of warm Army food. If you were in uniform anywhere in the world and could find an Army outfit, you would not go hungry. As I was leaving the mess hall, a clean-cut, young enlisted man walked up and confessed to being from my hometown. He had been in my younger sister's class. We visited for a few minutes, and I told him why I was there. He was not part of the Change of Command Ceremony but knew where the parade ground was and where Colonel Hard Ass would be. He escorted me to the grounds and filled me in as to what was going to happen. I thanked him more than was necessary. He had spent the last two months around the colonel and understood.

The ceremony was full of long speeches and long, straight rows of soldiers standing stalk-like in stifling heat. My job was simple: I was to be quiet and stay at least three paces behind the colonel at all times. I passed muster.

Immediately after the mandatory flyover of gunships and final salute to dismiss the troops, the colonel headed for his helicopter. I was welded three paces to his rear. The pilot had the engine warmed, and as soon as we were buckled up, he had us in the air.

The colonel was quiet on our flight back to my little home base. Pleased with the calm, I did nothing to change his mood. When we landed, he scowled mildly at me, and I knew I had been dismissed. There was no driver waiting for me. I pulled my olive drab baseball cap, with the Specialist 4th class insignia on the crown, tightly onto my pounding head and marched myself back to the protection of my company area.

I got to work early the next morning feeling like I had paid my debt to God, Country, Top, and the great good of The Order. The morning duties were easy—the sun was shining, life was good. Mid-morning, I looked up and saw Top coming into the treatment room. I had never seen nor heard of the man paying a visit to this work area, and it was soon obvious he was coming to see me. Now, I was confused and frightened. I could not remember doing anything so bad that I would face Court Martial. Before I could complete my inventory of bad things I had done in my life, Top was standing over me.

With no small talk preamble, he announced, "Tomorrow at 0800 hours, the Surgeon Commander of 15th Med will be here to take you with him for the day. This colonel is medical and new to the Battalion. It is important that you represent Charlie Company well." Top could pack a lot of anxiety and responsibility into a few words. I had no idea what to expect, but after my just completed day with a big boss, I was not comfortable or confident.

At 0745 the next morning, I presented myself at company headquarters as clean and militarily stiff as I could muster on short notice. To my surprise, I was met by a bubbling, thin Lt. Col. entertaining Top and my company clerk friend with college prank stories. The man had a flat-top military haircut and a face and body that I recognized immediately. I was standing face to face with Johnny Unitas, the great professional quarterback of the Baltimore Colts. I asked an innocent football question and knew instantly he was not Unitas and had little interest in football. I could not shake the image.

Johnny skipped all but basic military protocol. He excused himself from the office and drug me, a willing convert, to a helicopter that was waiting on the landing pad of our treatment facility. He took the co-pilot seat with an air of wonder and excitement, nothing like the sense of entitlement I had seen in the colonel of two days ago.

I pulled the flight helmet onto my head like an old-timer looking forward to real conversations. Johnny grew up the son of a small-town Midwest family doctor. His father was the kind of doctor who cured whatever his patients presented him. Johnny's uncles farmed the fields nearby. Johnny welcomed farm life and enjoyed the magic of his father's work. He shared both with delight.

Colonel Johnny had an appointment at his headquarters, which figured to take up part of the morning. Then, he was scheduled to meet with the Surgeon General of the Army at the General's office in Saigon. He delivered the mission as if I was always expected to be part of the party.

After that bit of housekeeping was complete, we talked farming. He had an interest in, and considerable knowledge of, the latest pesticides, herbicides, and even genetic research in grains. My knowledge was classroom and textbook. He had watched the crops with his uncles as they grew ripe in the field. The flight to his headquarters went much too quickly.

We left the helicopter and headed for his office with me, much like a collie pup at his heels. In his office, I found an empty chair near his clerk and was preparing to wait while he conducted business. He motioned me into his private office and put me in a chair. I watched quietly and reverently as he discussed military medical operations with the XOs of Companies A and B. I wondered why our XO was absent but did not ask.

He finished a peaceful workman-like meeting with his officers, grabbed his hat, and we headed back to the waiting helicopter. We were in sight of the plane when Johnny asked me if there was anything I needed from the headquarters company area. Much too boldly, I said I had been meaning to ask someone if I could have my vision checked. I read a lot and had been getting mild headaches after a long session with a book.

To my surprise, he made an abrupt about-face and said, "Follow me." Since everyone out-ranked me, and this man ranked somewhere near the Ozone Level, I got in step.

Johnny led me into a wood-frame building like most of the buildings on base, walked past the clerk on duty, and explained to the eye doctor in the back office that I might need some glasses to help with a reading habit, and we were in a bit of a hurry.

The eye doctor was a small person for an officer, and he seemed anxious to please my new favorite colonel. I was put in front of the eye-checking machine, and after a few questions about which letters I could read clearly, the little doctor said he thought my condition could be helped by a prescription pair of glasses. Johnny asked how long that might take and was told it would be early afternoon. Johnny said simply, "That will be fine."

I thanked the big colonel, and we left. To the Army, something that could be ready by mid-afternoon did not specify which mid-afternoon, so I didn't think much more about the eyewear.

The flight into Saigon was jaw-dropping. I had been through the town as part of a convoy in the cargo bed of an Army two-and-a-half-ton truck, universally called a deuce-and-a-half. From the ground, there is no way to appreciate the enormity and fertility of the rice paddy farmlands on the riverbanks near town.

On college field trips, I had driven through corn-growing land that seemed to spread forever. Compared to this, the corn fields back home were side-yard bean patches. Johnny had made this trip a few times, but his silence and reverence spoke loudly to his awe of the place.

We talked about the primitive methods these farmers used. There were no tractors. The few water buffalo working the fields were pulling plows older than the ones we have in the agriculture museums back home. Johnny and I agreed conservatively that the farms could produce three crops a year. The locals were bringing in one crop annually. With even a few modern tractors, they could double their yields. By the time we landed, we had hard figures proving the cropland we were seeing could feed the population of the entire world.

Johnny and I walked a short distance on pavement after we landed and then climbed a couple of flights of stairs. We stopped in front of a weather-beaten door that offered no clue that the room behind it housed a general of the U.S. Army.

Johnny knocked on the door, and a gruff voice said, "Come in." We did and were in the presence of General Thomas, Surgeon General of the U.S. war effort in Southeast Asia.

General Thomas vigorously shook Johnny's hand, and they broke into an animated conversation. I was not a part of that world, but for some reason, I didn't feel ignored. I am sure there must have been an important reason for Johnny's visit. It seemed more like a church social event to me. That image was crushed quickly when it became obvious that the curse words with which General Thomas began the meeting, and most every sentence thereafter were a large and important portion of his vocabulary.

The air in the general's office was heavy with cigar, pipe, and other smoke. There were a few hard-backed chairs in the room, but they went unused. The office was organized as I expected that of a general and doctor to be, and there were two walls of books in glass-covered cases. I have never been able to resist the urge to check the literature titles a person has around him. The first volumes I saw were exclusively on entomology. That seemed a little strange, but I figured he had a hobby. The books on the opposing wall were also about insects. I got a bit self-conscious and did not finish the inventory, but if there were human medical or military operations books, I did not see them.

Johnny had a big time and did introduce me, even explained to the general how I happened to be following him. General Thomas gave me a kindly once-over and went back to his visit. I decided it was unlikely he was related to any of my Thomas ancestors, so I did not mention the possibility.

There was a knock at the door, and two more high-ranking officers walked in. The chatter got louder, but I still did not hear anything military or medical in the conversation mix. Johnny decided he had fulfilled his mission, and, with so little military protocol that I missed it entirely, we left.

The flight back was peaceful. The rice fields looked even more majestic than they had on our flight in, and we felt comfortable staring silently.

When the pilot started bringing us down slowly, I began preparing some kind of thank you statement for the wonderful day. When we landed, I saw we were at 15th Med Headquarters, not Charlie Company. Johnny jumped to the ground and motioned me to catch up. He rushed me to the eye doctor's office, and, to my surprise, the doc had a pair of glasses with my name and prescription waiting. He put them on me and went through the doctor procedures to make sure they fit, and I could see as accurately as he thought good. Once he was satisfied, he presented me with the case and prescription in case I should want to replace them. Johnny thanked him and rushed me back to the chopper.

We landed on the Charlie Company pad just as the company was headed for the evening mess call. Johnny casually asked about the quality of our food. I was a little too confident by now and assured him that we might be in the wilds but that our mess crew was better than any in the U.S. Army. Johnny had been a part of the U.S. Army for a long time, and, to my surprise and fear, he asked to go with me to check it out for himself.

Our mess sergeant, known to all as Mess Daddy, was good. Mess Daddy was a tall, thin career staff sergeant who said little. No one asked him where or how he came up with the food we ate, and no one ever complained. It was good.

I was relieved and thankful when we entered the mess hall, and I saw spaghetti. The spaghetti Mess Daddy served was legendary—classic tomato sauce and cheese, sweet and tender meat. Rumor was that Mess Daddy traded in the local villages for fresh deer meat, some of which was surely killed by our helicopter pilots when they were checking out their repaired flight equipment.

Johnny followed me through the mess line and was at the table beside me, eating like he hadn't had a decent meal in months. Halfway through his meal, a couple of MDs came from their officer table, sat down, and started talking doctor. Johnny was comfortable with them. I thanked him again for letting me share his day and returned to the aid station to see what I had missed.

AARON

ALL THE MDS I served with in the war were draftees. They were all young, smart, and gifted. No two of the few I served closely with were at all alike. Dr. Aaron was a bit more different than the others. Doc Aaron was the last person you would expect to be in a military uniform. He was not tall. He was dumpy. He wore thick glasses, had an amble for a gait, and was not well-coordinated with his hands. He confessed to having been excused from the surgical rotation in med school, as any procedure past basic was beyond him. He had a superior mind that made up for any physical shortcomings, but among a bunch of athletic and handsome men, he stood out.

It was a rare occasion that Aaron wore his uniform with rank insignia and name. Most days, he was dressed as the rest of our medics—in a blue scrub shirt. He loved to do minor landscape projects around the company area. Most afternoons, while the other MDs were bumping and sweating on the company basketball court, Aaron was moving rock to make borders on our gravel paths.

One hot late afternoon, we were visited by a couple of military intelligence enlisted men who had a VC prisoner they wanted us to check out. The prisoner was a Lt. of some unit they named haughtily. The first person they met was Aaron, who was rearranging the rocks in front of our office. Aaron followed them in, and we started the examination.

The prisoner had been hit by a Claymore in both legs. The entry patterns were checkerboard like the textbook predicted of such a wound. He was far enough away from the mine that the projectiles penetrated only halfway into his legs. The wound had stopped bleeding by the time we saw him. The blood on his legs was clotted with red clay. The guards had the man stand up and walk into our facility. He walked with the stiffness of a man in great pain, but his facial expression showed only determination and strength. As soon as we had him in our facility, we got him on a litter and carried him to our treatment area.

Aaron took charge of his treatment immediately. He wanted to get fluid into the man and check for other wounds. The guards only wanted to know if he would live long enough for them to question him. A struggle of will broke out, and the guards said they were taking him with them. Aaron tried to pull rank, but he had no insignia on him. Fortunately, we had an E6 in the office on other business, and he bailed us out. The guards left, and we started treating the prisoner.

Aaron thought there might be more trouble, so he rushed to his hootch, got his clean captain uniform on, and came back to help us. We got an IV into the man and started cleaning the leg wounds. Before we were finished, the guard returned with a member of their staff who sported a second Lt. bar. Aaron was now prepared to block that threat. Again, the intelligence men left, and we worked more quickly.

We got all the fluid we could get into the man and bandaged the major parts of his legs. Well before Aaron was satisfied that we had done our duty, the G2 crew returned with a major and threatened to remove the man by force. We could only stand and watch as they forced the prisoner to walk to the jeep they had waiting.

THE PISTOL

IN APRIL 1970, the Binh Long Province of the Republic of South Vietnam saw rain every day. At 1400 hours every afternoon, we watched lightning trails appear in an otherwise clear sky. The streaks were so high that if thunder was chasing them, we mortals could not hear it.

Six minutes after the silent fireworks, a localized cloud rolled up, dark and low. The cloud bank was so slow it did not present a sense of panic—it presented foreboding. Once the shroud had covered us, we were completely at her mercy.

It was so dark inside the cloud we could not see. Then the drizzle started. Gradually, the raindrops became as intense as the discharge of a large waterfall. Every living and dormant thing within her reach was soaked, slippery, slimy, and cold.

There was an element of peace within the storm. Enemy and friendly alike were wedded to their positions. No one shuffled to a stronger location. The fortunate listened to the music of giant raindrops drumming the sheet metal roof and thought of home. Those outside, shivering, bunched under OD ponchos, cursed the cold and waited for the slug-like storm to visit elsewhere.

My little group of medical professionals spent this particular weather event listening to the more cerebral member impress the three others and the captive audience with his memorized knowledge of the medical wisdom printed in the 1968 edition of *The Merck Manual*. The other enlisted medic and I each had a copy of the book, and we were determined to find a passage or obscure fact this show-off did not know. The other MD sat by, bored.

We were soon throwing random page numbers at Super Doc and getting awfully tired of hearing him quote word-for-word to

David Rozzell

include footnotes and references when the clerk came to us with word that one of our medevac helicopters was on the way with the remains from a downed helicopter.

Remains and downed helicopter were not words we liked to hear in the same sentence. We got all the equipment together to cover any problem, but there was no preparation for what came.

The helicopter and its package came softly onto our landing pad just as the weather front was making its way out, rain still weakly falling, and the afternoon sun returning without apology.

Our four-man company of specialists scrambled to the incoming chopper in our practiced, professional, and prepared way. In the hold of that ship, we found a tarp covering the floor and then folded neatly to conceal the offering we were receiving. It was painfully obvious the only living forms on that ship were the men of our medevac crew.

Before the whirl of the main rotor was stilled, the buildings of our medical company spewed so many men to our side that lifting the bundle to the flat surface of our landing pad seemed much too easy. Six body bags appeared and were orderly placed, unzipped, to the side of the tarp nearest the morgue. Four long-handle shovels appeared at the top of the body bags.

Bad news travels unchecked in a closed and tightly-packed community like an Army firebase. Word had leaked that the downed bird was in a remote, rugged mountainside, and what was left of the helicopter was spread over a large area of boulders, cliffs, and trees.

By the time we got the equipment deployed and a plan of attack established for recording the human aspect of the horrid event in a manner satisfactory to the U.S. Army and, in some small way, the family and loved ones of these men, we had collected a large congregation. Most of the members were our family—the cook staff in their white coats and no caps, some of the motor pool bunch with oil grime permanent black stains under their nails, the helicopter crew huddled near the nose of the big flying machine still wearing their flight helmets with eye shields activated. It seemed like most of the off-duty men in the vicinity of our company area were present or represented, and there were as many mumbled explanations concerning the wreck as there were men. The weather was given her due.

The tarp had four corners, and since there were four members of our team, we each grabbed a corner. We unfolded the tarpaulin smoothly until its full surface was flat on our pad. Then, we got our first look at the remains.

It was far more gruesome and horrible than we could have expected and yet contained less physical human matter. I was reminded of the final cleanup stages of my farmer neighbor's hog butchering, just without the cold weather and the hot water boiling in a big cast iron kettle. I learned young in life to find important things I needed to do elsewhere when words like butchering were mentioned.

Our immediate team—me, the ranking enlisted medic, and the two captain MDs—had been exposed to gore for months, but this carnage stopped all activity. We looked at each other with quick glances, hoping someone else would start the dreaded processing, but not even Super Doc spoke up. Finally, we gave in to the weight of our certain fate and began to work. We did not comment on it til much later, but each of us knew that, by this point in the proceedings, our audience was long gone.

We were fortunate enough to have the dog tags of each individual and started things out by assigning a dog tag to each body bag. We slugged through the remains, searching for shards we could positively tie to one of our deceased friends. There were six flight helmets, and with some detective work, we placed the correct one in each bag. There were nine boots. Each member of the fated party got one in hopes it was his. They shared the others. What bits of uniform we could reasonably assume belonged to an individual went with him. The final distribution of matter we carefully, and with all dignity and reverence we could muster, divided into six equal piles using the shovels. Then, we shoveled the contents of each pile into a bag.

Near the bottom of the excavation, I found a pistol. Usually, the weapons of a casualty were collected by the ranking soldier on site. That man was responsible for getting the now-unassigned tool back into the system. If a rifle or pistol disappeared in normal war activity, the appropriate DD form was filed by the supply master, and the weapon was dumped into the Army purgatory known as "combat loss." We had helped several pistols find new life after combat hell. I noticed nothing unusual about this model 1911 Colt .45 cal pistol, so the senior enlisted medic and I started the process.

Mr. Zip, our battalion's favorite medevac helicopter pilot, was soon returning to the States and a new life, so we got tenuous approval from the MDs in our midst, cleaned the pistol somewhat, and went directly to the pilot billet. I offered the pistol to Zip with a brief history. He thanked me. We went back to the treatment facility, thinking that was the end of the story.

The next morning, near the end of sick call, I noticed a normal-sized man in the perfectly fitted uniform of an officer storm through the door to our clerk. His whole bearing said, "I am important, I am on a mission, I am not happy, and you lowlifes better have some news for me very quickly."

This unhappy man found our company commander, who was the kindest, most caring, healing sort of medicine man I ever met, and gave him a loud dressing down heard by everyone in the facility. Our CO gave him an innocent look and somehow convinced the rude man to stand down for a minute.

The CO came to my desk and gently drug me out of the room. He patiently explained that the colonel was led to believe that someone in our unit had stolen a pistol from the medevac ship that recovered the body of a general officer who went down with the helicopter. It seems this particular pistol had been given to the general by his father, who had carried the pistol through all of WWII, and the family really wanted to have it back. The CO looked much too directly into my eyes and said, "You know anything about this, Doc?"

Troubled Sleep

I was never much good when it came to lying. Nobody lied to this man anyhow. I told him I would be right back. Then I double-timed it to the pilot quarters and spilled my guts at the feet of Mr. Zip, who was listening to some music in cut-off shorts and a t-shirt. Zip looked at me, grinned, and said, "I'll take care of it."

I ambled back to the treatment room with the cares of life lifted from my body. I told the CO that Mr. Zip had the gun and was on his way over to clean things up. The CO went to assure the colonel. I found an unused desk as close to the action as I dared and waited.

By the time I found a pen and some random paperwork to scratch on, Mr. Zip walked through the open entry door we used to transport wounded patients from incoming medevac ships. The sun glared off his uniform. Zip shined like my dad thought his car should. His boots must have been patent leather. His belt buckle gleamed like a mirror. He had medals I had never seen before, and I was not at all sure how he could have earned them.

Mr. Zip walked in, and his footsteps made a crisp, loud rhythm a tap dancer would be proud of. Yet he appeared for all the world to be gliding inches off the floor. He had a dress hat of some kind, and the instant his head cleared the door jamb, he snapped the thing off his head with his left hand and cradled it smartly to his side.

His march ended at a perfect three-feet six-inches in front of the colonel. Zip performed a textbook halt and salute with the required, "Mr. Zip reporting, Sir." Zip held the salute until the now-disarmed officer returned it. Zip reached behind his back, retrieved the pistol in his right hand, and presented it to the officer. He apologized for not getting the pistol back in the system sooner, saying simply he had been flying rescue missions most of the night, and assured the big shot officer that the safety and security of the pistol had been uppermost in his plans at all times.

The colonel took the pistol and thanked Zip. Before there could develop any embarrassment between them, Zip snapped a salute, and the instant it was acknowledged, he did a stunning about-face and left the building as he had come.

The colonel thanked our commander in a much quieter manner than he had entered with, and then he and his bodyguards slunk out by way of the clerk's office.

The tight little group of medical experts who were in the audience for Zip's performance were graveyard quiet after the officer left. As soon as the offensive man and his goons were out of the company area, the front desk clerk rushed into the room and flashed the all-clear sign, which was followed by a few minutes of loud clapping, cheers, whistles, and inappropriate laughter.

RED

LATE ONE MORNING, early in my tour with the 1st Cav, we got a call from the medevac crew assigned to us. They had taken fire, and Red, their left door gunner, had been hit. They were ten minutes out and wanted everybody ready.

We quickly got everything ready, rounded up all the medical doctors, and listened for updates. There was no more radio contact from our incoming patient.

When the initial call came in, our nosey radio operator learned that the helicopter had made a routine delivery of a field medic to a nearby fire support base and had taken sniper fire as they left the camp. Since we heard nothing else from them, we did all the "'what ifs," got ready to call up another medevac ship, and got ready for more casualties in our treatment facility.

The 1st Cav operated their medevac program a bit differently because one of the first commanders had decided he knew how to do things better. The Cav had their own pilots, choppers, and medics, and they were armed.

The pilots, crew chiefs, and medics were part of the Cav and had volunteered to do the hard jobs that came with it. The door gunners were different. It seemed to me they must have been taken from a redneck bar fight somewhere. Nothing scared those guys. If there was not a fight for them to get into every few days, they were hard to live with.

Red was the meanest. He was not a redhead, and I always wondered where the name came from. No one I asked seemed to know, and I was not brave enough to ask the man himself. I could not imagine any VC brave enough to shoot at him.

At exactly ten minutes after we got the call, the helicopter carrying Red sat down softly on our landing pad. Red was the first crew member off the chopper. His head and the front of his upper body were covered with reddish material that could have been blood. As he got closer, it became obvious that it was not. Red was covered with a dark, sticky baked bean sauce.

Door gunners, and I guess all machine gunners, were constantly adding improvements to their machine guns to make sure they operated smoothly. Red had found a can of baked beans that was the perfect size to feed the ammo belt up and directly into the machine gun. That sniper made a direct hit to Red's can of hot bean sauce, and it covered his face and body.

We were never sure who was the most frightened by the results, and unlike most incidents of this nature, no one laughed or gave Red any grief about it.

We did not offer to clean him up.

THE DEAN

EARLY IN MY stay with the 1st Cav, our company became temporary quarters for a special doctor. The rumor was that this doctor wanted to see how the medevac method of getting wounded from the field and to treatment quickly actually worked. He took a leave of absence from his job as the dean of a medical school in Ohio and got the Army to give him the temporary rank of colonel and short-term assignments to first-line medevac units.

He was sent to our unit as his first assignment. I did not get a chance to ask him how many of the rumors about his mission were accurate. The Dean stayed with us only a few weeks, but the man packed far more experience than that into his stay.

The Dean moved in with the doctors but spent most of his days and nights with the medevac crew. Where they went, he went. He kept a recording device running constantly. Much of the audio had to be deleted for the excessive use of curse words. The pilots assured us he was much worse than they were.

The Dean would come off the helicopter first, holding the front handles of the stretcher. Then, he would wait impatiently for one of us mortals to get the other end and help him move the patient into the treatment room. More often than not, he had the treatment underway as the crew flew in. If he did not have the instruments to treat the patient, he called in and had us ready what was needed.

One afternoon, we had a soldier who had fallen, or been pushed, into a mud bank. His airway was blocked. The simple processes we used to clear such obstructions were not working. A tracheotomy had to be done. I had seen a few of these performed. They were slow and required cutting back layers of skin and subcutaneous material until you found the trachea. Once that was done, a hole was cut into the trachea, and a tube was inserted.

The Dean was walking through at the time. He saw the situation and took over. He prepped and draped the area in one movement, then picked up a scalpel and, with the smoothest move I ever saw, cut the flesh to the trachea. He cut the trachea and retracted it. The patient was breathing instantly. He left the closure to Dr. Martin. The Dean patted the patient gently on the shoulder, removed his gloves, and left with the flight crew.

Later that week, our medevac crew, with The Dean on board, picked up the pilot of a downed Cobra. The Dean called in and requested the presence of the whole medical team. The pilot had lost a lot of blood, and The Dean wanted us to have all the supplies we had ready to use.

We got the pilot into the treatment room with The Dean working on him non-stop. He had been doing external heart massage the whole trip in. He turned that job over to Dr. Martin and started putting blood into the man.

The Dean was monitoring the blood pressure cuff, checking for a heartbeat, and urging more blood into the pilot with the energy of a freestyle gymnast. We all tried to help, and not get in the way at the same time.

We put all the blood we had in the aid station into the man and were still getting no positive response. At that point, The Dean slowed down and said the only thing left was to try internal heart massage. Without blinking or drawing a guideline, he grabbed the scalpel on the instrument tray and made an eight-inch incision into the man's skin. With a second stroke, he opened the chest cavity. The blood we had been putting into the pilot had pooled in his abdomen.

In what seemed like one continuous move, The Dean put his right hand into the man's chest and started gently massaging the man's heart. It became obvious we had lost the man, and The Dean became the professor. He inserted his hand into the chest and quickly found the reason we were making no progress. The aorta had split from the trauma of the crash.

The Dean asked each doctor to practice the heart massage techniques. Dr. Martin started the rotation. He put his hand in and started to massage the heart. Dean stopped him. He explained that Dr. Martin was "a repentant member of the thumb through the left ventricle club." He said, "The thumb should never be on the inside of the chest while performing internal heart massage."

He patiently worked with each doctor. Before I could stop myself, I asked to be included. The Dean walked me through the process as if I were one of his surgical students. He asked that I check out the aorta. I was amazed. The vessel was the size of a three-quarter-inch garden hose. The split was three inches long and as smooth as one of The Dean's incisions.

I found myself anxious to learn more from The Dean. It was obvious that every man in the company was.

The next morning, he left our company and joined an evac hospital.

BRACED

EARLY MORNING ON the second day of the Cambodian invasion, we had a colonel of the ARVN military brought to our aid station. It was claimed he had been in the middle of a heated gunfire exchange between the ARVN regulars and a large group of NVA regulars on the Ho Chi Minh Trail. This colonel was named Hoe. He was standard height for the citizens of South Vietnam, but his body type and skin color were more that of the Pillsbury Doughboy. He was surrounded by uniformed men with proportions more consistent with the civilians we saw every day, and they were protective of the colonel, who was whining pitifully.

The wound was on the back of the colonel's pasty fat calf, and the blood from it covered maybe six inches square and had dried. We carefully cut the starched uniform to find a small puncture wound like we often saw from shrapnel. In deference to the man's rank, our senior medical doctor handled the treatment. He gently probed the wound and then softly removed a piece of shrapnel from it. He personally cleaned the area and bandaged it. We were able to quickly get a helicopter to take the colonel and his men to the nearest evac hospital for follow-up.

It was a busy time, and none of us had slept in forty-eight hours, so there was not a big deal made of the situation. I sat on the waiting room bench, leaned against the timber building support, and thought to grab a nap. One of our doctors was already occupying the other side of the post, and I thought he was asleep. This doctor was a southern boy who had done undergrad at Davidson College when ROTC was required of all students. All the staff members wore blue scrub shirts while on duty, and his had gone unwashed for a little longer than mine, but I didn't complain.

I had just gotten comfortable when someone walked up behind me and asked, "Has Colonel Hoe been treated here this morning?" It was not an unusual question, and without turning to look, I said, "Yeah, we treated him an hour ago and sent him to Saigon."

At this point, the roof lifted off the treatment facility, and the voice of God himself said, "Do you know who I am? You stand at attention when you are in my presence!" I set the world speed record for waking up, standing, and bracing against the wall. Somehow, from the corner of my eyes, which were also fixed at attention, I noticed two big stars on the man's uniform. I guess he realized quickly I was not about to respond anymore, and obviously didn't know any more because he turned and left the facility.

I was passively aware of my buddy, the medical doctor, throughout the ordeal, plastered against the wall in the same brace I had assumed. As soon as the General was out of sight, I backhanded the man and asked why he, the big Captain Officer, left me, the lowly enlisted man, to deal with the big man. My friend laughed and said, "Looked to me like you had everything under control."

KID

TWO WEEKS AFTER the Cambodian invasion, all the extra troops moved back to where they came from. Our sick calls were so light that we were sitting around looking at each other most of the time, reading or discussing whatever the officer with the loudest voice wanted to talk about.

Our company found ways to restructure and keep peace. During the wait for orders from on high, our leadership allowed every member of the company to pursue the things they felt were important. In the treatment area, we cut down the hours each of us spent on duty.

Sundays, even before the invasion, were quiet, and the aid station was lightly manned with a backup crew ready. On the second Sunday following the end of the big battle, I found myself in charge of the station with a medic I knew only from seeing him in the ward. We spoke a little, and he went to a corner and started reading a book. I did what prep work I thought was necessary and did a routine check of the meds we kept on our treatment shelf. They were always getting out of order or not replaced at all.

I was nearly to the last shelf on that Sunday when a soldier walked in, leading a ten-year-old Vietnamese boy. The soldier came back to me and contemptuously explained that he had seen this kid rooting through the dump when he was emptying his truck on a routine trash run. He said the kid had talked back to one of the soldiers who was removing trash, and the soldier had thrown a brick and hit the kid in the head.

I took the boy's hand and led him to the treatment area. I heard all my life about being "scared stiff." This boy was the poster child for the term.

When I got the child on a litter and got the dirty rag off the wound on his head, I found a cut of eight inches, which went all the way to his skull. I had never seen the skull of a human being. The bleeding had stopped, and the wound was not as dirty as I had feared, but piecing the layers back together was going to take some time. I knew we would never see the kid again, so keeping possible infection down bothered me.

I asked the medic who was with me if he would clean the wound and prep it while I gathered the suture materials, gloves, and instruments I would need to close it.

He shrugged indifferently. When I came back to the boy, I found my helper back in his corner with his book and my patient only half-prepared. I cleaned the wound much more thoroughly than I would have otherwise and got the wound draped. The child was so traumatized that I did not even deaden the skin.

Head wounds are simple as wound closures go. I had never seen the skull before, but there was a clear membrane that had to be closed first. After that, it was a simple matter of closing the middle layer and then the skin, each tightly enough so that no loose portions were left that could collect infection. I got the skin closed as tightly as I dared and then stepped back and inspected my handiwork.

I asked my assistant if he would mind putting a bandage on the finished product while I got the little bit of required paperwork done.

The man did not bother to look up or answer. By this time, I was getting a bit put out with my helper and said something mildly inappropriate.

My fellow medic said, "Damn, Doc. What's the big deal? He's just a Gook kid."

All conversation with the medic ended. I covered the wound and gently led him back to the front of the bunker to wait for a ride home. The boy was still frightened, but I felt confident his wound would heal. In the remaining months of my tour, I found the same attitude in places I did not expect to find it. I never understood it nor learned to gracefully accept it.

RABIES

THERE WERE NO doors on the bunker which housed our treatment room. As with most things military, I never questioned why. It did make it easier for the wounded to get quickly to our doctors and medics. The weather was never cold, so there was no reason to keep the heat in. The perimeter of the base camp was well-defended, so the enemy was not likely to wander in. We did sometimes have visitors late into the night. The MPs were our most consistent night visitors. They would say they were patrolling and wanted to make sure we were ok. They would stand around and talk for an hour or so, then go back into the dark.

One bright night, well before midnight, a mob of soldiers swarmed through the back entrance of our treatment room. There were at least a dozen of them. They looked like they had been involved in a mud wrestling event in a dry gravel parking lot. They were carrying something which was making as much noise as they were.

When the dust settled, I saw that the something they were all gathered around was a human. A very angry human.

He was a large man. At home, we would have called him a corn-fed, farmboy type. The battle this squad had been in was now obvious. The man they had physically subdued was secured between two carry litters. There was enough rope tied to the ends and around the litters and man to supply a good ranch.

The secured man was the most wild-eyed, deranged-looking individual I had ever seen. I asked everyone who would talk about what caused the episode, but no one seemed to know. They did not think the man was into drugs, and the word rabies was mentioned more than once. The only thing the patient would say was, "Screw the lifers." When he said it, I thought for sure the devil was going to appear from underneath the building and do a number on all of us.

The clerk called the charge doctor, who was there instantly. He took in the situation and drew up a dose of Thorazine. The doctor handed it to me and told me to get the med into his arm. I was not excited about getting that close to the man, but I calmly eased the needle into an exposed arm and plunged the meds into him.

I was shocked to see there was no reaction. By the time I had gotten out of harm's way, the man went even more berserk than before. The gathering watched, dumbfounded, for a few minutes, and then the drug took effect, and we had a calm patient.

The leader of the attending herd gave us what information we needed to move the patient to a facility better equipped to care for him, and the horde vanished. Within the hour, we had an in-house helicopter take the still-hog-tied patient to an evac hospital.

That night, I did not sleep. I sat in my break-down chair in the corner far from the entrance and read til my shift ended and breakfast called.

DON

OUR MEDICAL COMPANY staff included a diverse group of men. One of my favorites was a youngster named Don. In my first conversation with him, he described himself as an entrepreneur. The thing that came to my mind was an aggressive businessperson, but I went to the dictionary in our day room and found it was an individual who is "action-oriented, who can deftly navigate whatever is in front of him." That was Don.

Don was qualified to be a good field medic. He saw the problems with being in the middle of combat and decided it would be safer in the rear. He had many skills and made himself necessary to Top, the person who decided where a person worked. Don had also learned to perform the lab work necessary to keep things moving at the aid station. He claimed to have spent a year or so, while in college in Ohio, working nights at the local hospital where he learned the trade.

He did all the little construction jobs Top wanted in his office and hootch. Somehow, Don knew when the resupply planes were coming in and would be there with a crew to break down the wood crates and bring them back to the company area so he could keep a ready supply of construction materials. I know this because I was the first lumber hauler he called. He took a lot of heat for being a "bootlicker," "toady," and "brown noser." I heard him say more than once that he "was not ashamed to be Top's biggest suck-up if it kept him in the rear and safe."

We had a bright local female who worked in the company area. Don liked to be around her and spent time teaching her nursing skills so she could have a better life than sweeping the company area and polishing boots. One afternoon, Don had just finished mixing a stain for testing malaria and needed some blood to make sure it worked properly. He reasoned his girl was far enough into her training to draw a little blood, so he volunteered his arm and showed her the basics of tourniquet application and where to find the vein.

Don turned his head in case the needle stick was more painful than he had planned. He felt a soft prick and thought he was indeed an exceptional trainer. He looked around to make sure the rest of the procedure went as planned. His eyes got to the needle just in time to see 10 cc of air pumped into his waiting vein.

The news of this event spread quickly, and as soon as I could finish my sick call duties, I rushed to his office area to check on him. In training, we spent a lot of time expelling the air from a syringe so that not even a bubble of air was put into a body when we administered a shot. Don had not been brought to the aid station, so I figured he survived, but I sure wanted to know first-hand about the damage.

When I got to Don, he was as white as any ghost but standing. I asked, of course, what it felt like, and he said, "Like being hit full in the chest by a team of sledgehammers."

X-RAY BOSS

AT 0770 HOURS, Don gently shook me awake and told me I was needed in the treatment room. For the last few weeks, it had not been uncommon for me to be called. X-ray Boss was now a short-timer, and once he knew I would and could take x-rays in his absence, he tended to be absent a lot.

I got to the treatment area to find a room full of wounded. The patient was stable—a staff sergeant with a chest wound the doctors were concerned about. Dr. Martin thought he may have bled in the chest cavity and collapsed a lung and wanted an x-ray to confirm things before doing any further treatment.

This x-ray was the most common we did and was pretty foolproof. All we were looking for was a clear image to confirm the lungs were inflated. I set the machine without worrying about perfection and triggered the device.

I left the staff sergeant in the x-ray area in case something went wrong with my efforts. I quickly put the film through the developing procedure and, as soon as I got it out of the dip tank, took it, still dripping, to Dr. Martin. Martin saw that the lungs were clear and in no danger of collapsing, so he securely bandaged the staff sergeant and issued orders to get him to the evac hospital.

Dr. Martin asked for the film again and called the group around. The film was not dry but set enough to see the distinct image of a bullet in the middle of the heart. We talked about how, in a body cavity, the bullet was probably behind the heart and just lined up to look like it was inside from the angle I took the picture. We had a good talk and laugh, and I took the film back into the x-ray area so it could finish drying and went back to bed.

A week or so later, we had finished sick call, and as we were cleaning up, Don walked into the area. He had been to mail call and was carrying a letter from his mother. She had enclosed a newspaper clipping from a town near her. The article was about a staff sergeant from that town who was in Vietnam and was on his way home after being wounded.

The article explained how the sergeant had been shot in the heart, and the bullet had lodged in the wall separating the right and left chambers of the heart. The bullet had been traveling at just the right speed. It stopped there and kept the heart from bleeding out. The article was also specific enough as to the date of the wound, the unit of the sergeant, and the area his unit was serving that we had no doubt it was the sergeant we treated.

X-ray Boss quickly disappeared into his private room and returned with the dry and finished film. He showed the radiograph to all of us and, in his most arrogant and learned voice, explained how perfect the detail of the heart was and how perfectly the heart and the projectile were centered. He was just ready to tell us how lucky we were to have him in our midst.

Dr. Martin broke in softly, looked at me, and said, "Doc, that's the film you took of the big blond staff sergeant to check for a hemothorax, isn't it?"

I nodded.

X-ray Boss grabbed the film and walked out of the room, pitching it in the trash as he passed.

BUGS

MY FRIEND DON, the entrepreneur and med tech, spent a lot of time with me during the few months he was part of our company. He always needed my help when there was heavy lifting to be done, and he knew I would listen to his many zany ideas for making a quick buck. I loved to talk to someone about home and work that was not related to war.

Don shared many schemes with me. He had a cousin who was doing house construction, and Don hoped to work with him to construct a complex of apartment buildings and live the life of the rich and famous.

His cousin wrote often and must have been of the same mind. One day, he came to me with a letter from his cousin, saying he needed my help with a foolproof project that would bring us some real money. His cousin had run into someone in the research division of his local college who was interested in unusual and hard-to-find insects and reptiles. His cousin reasoned that Vietnam was as far away a land as there was, and since we were already there and in the jungle where such animals lived, we could supply them.

I am afraid of snakes, so I drew the line there. But we fought insects all day, every day, and there were some strange ones. I never bothered to get to know any of them or their origin and really hated the monster mosquitoes, but the other bugs were just bugs. We spent a week or two studying the different species on hand and caught a few to see how difficult that would be.

Don paid a visit to the post mail office and found we could indeed ship insects back to the States if we preserved them properly and filled out paperwork stating that they would be used for research.

Don had access to the chemicals from his company lab, and we found pins and packaging that would satisfy the post office. We were in business. The only chemical we needed was formaldehyde, and we had a ready supply of that. It was simply a matter of gathering 10 cc syringes and large needles from combat loss. We started collecting bugs.

The first batch were big. We didn't know the scientific name yet, but there were geeks in our ward who would know such things. We got the formaldehyde and needles and set up a table. I was doing a lot of surgery at the time, so I got to hold the syringe and apply the formaldehyde to the softest part of the insect.

Things were going well the first day, and we were feeling more confident by the minute. The next afternoon, we encountered an especially tough-skinned insect. Don was holding it down with effort, and I was doing my "if you push harder, it will solve all problems" solution to all things difficult. It didn't. I was pushing the plunger of the syringe, as well as the syringe, and the formaldehyde separated the needle and blew the full 10 cc of formaldehyde into Don's right eye.

Fearing the absolute worst, I ran to the aid station, grabbed the first doctor I saw, and told him my story. He managed to make me feel like a complete idiot without saying so and told me to rinse the eye with saline solution for five minutes. If that did not help, we would have to send Don to the evac hospital.

I grabbed two bags of solution and application tubes and put Don in a chair with his head back while I ran the two bags through his eye, then went back for two more. He was not happy with me for using so much fluid, but the next morning, his eye was fine. We did not discuss it but did not continue the bug project.

FOOD

DON WAS NOT a conscientious objector. We never talked about such things, but he kept his M16 clean and serviceable, just like we all did. He carried the thing with him when on post, as was required, and always presented it in good working order when we were inspected. However, he never fired the thing and would not go on the gun runs we often took with the medevac crews.

He was not as easy to put into a personality type as some of the rest. He kept to himself yet was always part of everything. Don was always ahead of us. He had many far-reaching ideas and plans, but one thing surprised me. He never talked of taking up the restaurant business.

I was never a big food-for-fun person, but Don showed me things I would not have considered. He was a frequent visitor to the local Vietnamese village community bread ovens. He would come back to base with rice bread still warm from those ovens. Somehow, he would also have butter, and I have never tasted any bread to match it.

Where he came up with the butter is another matter. Mess Daddy was wonderful and a master at getting us food and preparing it to perfection. I never saw him conspiring with Don, but that is the magic of conspiracy. Don would be gone some nights near midnight and come back bearing gifts. One night, he brought in a half-gallon of vanilla ice cream. I do not remember it being served at the mess hall at any time.

We had the best meats in the country, and word was that he traded in the village and that the medevac crews often took fresh-killed deer to the village to exchange for good water buffalo. We never questioned his methods.

Don's specialty was soups, prepared in his popcorn maker. I never saw a cooking device like it before or after. The popping bowl lifted from the heating element and doubled as a serving device or a communal eating plate. His mother sent popcorn. It was difficult to hide the popping noise from our neighbors, who somehow showed up soon after a bowl was ready to eat.

Most of the things he prepared I had some knowledge of, but he came in one night with a handful of oysters. I had never seen one, and they looked utterly disgusting. Don put the slimy things in his popper and added milk. I have no idea how he got the milk, but then he added way too much butter, salt, and pepper, and something new to me. He put the heat to that cooker and stirred it for a while. The smell was wonderful, and I was soon hungry enough to at least taste it. Without a doubt, that was the most wonderful meal I ever had.

RUNS

A FEW WEEKS after the rains stopped, our sick calls started to bring in more than the usual cases of diarrhea. Our second-in-command medical doctor had practiced in areas where such things were common, and he diagnosed the problem quickly.

We were seeing an outbreak of Shigella. Shigella is a bacterial organism that does bad things to the human digestive system. The patients who showed up in our clinic presented with a horrible case of "the shits."

Of course, there are other things that cause the bowels to run, so we were asked to prove the presence of the Shigella organism before we started a full assault on that specific bug. My friend Don was asked to get that proof. That meant Don had to collect fecal specimens from some of the sick men and run cultures looking for the specific Shigella bacteria.

Don had to do some research, as he had never heard of the organism, but that was easy enough. Collecting stool samples was easy since we had a pretty big pool of men shedding the thing, so within twenty-four hours, he was able to prove, to the satisfaction of the doctors, that Shigella was what we were dealing with.

The treatment for most forms of diarrhea is rest, plenty of fluids, and letting the body fight it off. This outbreak was different. Within two days, it had spread through so many of our troops that a whole battalion of the 1st Cav had to be taken out of the field. More of these guys than we normally see in the course of a day at our aid station came by asking for help. For the most part, we were supportive and, in the worst cases, administered antibiotic injections.

All the members of our medical team were on call day and night and did not contract the disease. Don, however, got an early and severe case of the illness. He had cramps so bad that, for most of the three days and nights, he slept in our company jeep a few feet from the latrine. I brought him water and whatever the mess hall had that he felt he could eat. I also gave him a steady diet of kidding about being so wimpy.

Don recovered and was back to work and sleeping in the hootch we shared. Everything calmed down, and the battalion went back into the field.

The night after everything settled down, I woke up around 3 o'clock in the morning feeling a strange but urgent call to the latrine. I walked as fast as I could the fifty feet to the two-holer and almost made it before the cutoff fatigue pants I slept in filled with warm liquid fecal material. I was close to the perimeter wire, so I pulled the smelly things off and threw them over the barbed wire. I slunk to the shower and cleaned the evidence off my lower body parts. Then I sneaked back to the hootch.

Don lay there looking at me and said, "It got you, didn't it." The next morning, I was prepared for the major harassment I deserved, but Don never mentioned the situation.

DJ

IN THE SPRING of 1970, the Army sent a young man to our base camp near Quan Loi to entertain us. Most of the men had a radio of some description, but there was no live broadcast until DJ James came to us.

The camp was not that large, so from the day he set up his turntable and microphone, he was the most listened-to man on base. He was live from eight a.m. until six p.m. On Sunday, since he was a one-man show, he took liberties with the schedule.

The first few weeks, DJ talked very little and played music he liked or thought we all liked. Soon, the guys on base found out how to contact him and would request their favorites. With men from every part of the U.S., there was diversity, to say the least, and if DJ admitted to not having a particular selection, it quickly showed up at his shop. He grew into the job quickly, and soon, his chatter was as entertaining as the music.

DJ managed to keep the location of his office secret for the most part. One of our medics discovered his place, and our company became frequent visitors. The broadcast shack was a sheet metal roofed-and-sided deal not one hundred yards from our aid station. DJ had a wooden table, his turntable squarely in front of him, his microphone in his left hand, and his records and notes to the right. It was simple and, like all things on base, covered with red dust, but he managed to make it work.

We had a radio in our aid station and routinely listened to DJ as we did morning sick call. One Friday morning, we heard incoming mortars close to the treatment bunker. DJ's broadcast went immediately dead. All the medics in the aid station ran toward the broadcast hut. I was closest to the building, so I got to the hut as two of my friends pulled open the door.

Inside, we found a hole in the thin sheet metal roof just over his head and saw the record he had been playing smashed all over the room. Behind his desk sat a ghostly white DJ, who would not move. His eyes, however, were wild, wide, and wanting to talk. I got closer and asked him where he was hit. His eyes moved down toward his legs. I followed them to an unexploded mortar round lodged in the seat of his chair nestled quietly between his thighs.

Explosions in a war zone always draw a crowd. Fortunately, this event brought a man who knew mortars. We watched in awe as he gently picked up the deadly thing and carried it off. The power to trust life and limb to the ability of a total stranger during war is unbelievable. Fortunately, the bomb did not detonate.

My always-in-the-right-place friend Don knew enough to have driven the ambulance with supplies and litter to the site. We picked DJ up, put him in the front seat of the jeep, and took him to the treatment room. There was not even a scratch on the man.

I kept him in the aid station overnight and released him the next morning to hunt replacement equipment for his job.

MUSTACHE

JUST BEFORE TOTAL darkness set in, a few mortar rounds dropped on the green line not far from our treatment bunker. I was on duty with a support group of one new-in-country medic. When I got to the rear entrance of our bunker, I saw several wounded men headed toward us. I sent my helper to the clerk with orders to call in the MDs and what aid men he could. Our clerk had already called in reinforcements.

We kept four litters set up and ready for treatment at all times, and they quickly filled. All our doctors were on hand and treating the wounded. The rush had pretty much ended when I noticed a couple of men walk into the aid station.

One was leaning on the other, so I took him to the rear of the room and sat down to check him. The wounded man had been close to the main wall of the base camp, and a mortar had exploded just on the other side of the wall from him. His friend confirmed that the explosion had knocked him down pretty hard.

His vital signs were normal, so I grabbed Dr. Martin and explained the situation. Dr. Martin told me that, from the bloated stomach, the man probably had gotten internal damage, but if his blood pressure remained normal, he would be safe to send on to the evac hospital. He said that, unlike the chest wall and muscle groups, the stomach was able, in most cases, to block the bleeding vessels and maintain the blood pressure until we could get him to better care.

I was ordered to prepare the paperwork fixed to move him and to keep him as calm as possible until the transport helicopter arrived. I set up a litter near the back wall and went to see what help I could be with the other wounded.

Earlier that week, we had taken in a medical doctor. He told us he had been with one of the evac hospitals for a few months and wanted to see how things were on the front lines. The man could wear a uniform. He was clean, pressed, polished, and loud. His face was perfectly tanned, well-proportioned, and set off with the blackest, thickest head of hair I'd ever seen. The focal point was a mustache—full, black, and combed. The ends were turned up perfectly and must have been held that way by some magic glue.

I had been attempting to grow a mustache my entire stay in-country, and it looked, at best, like I had milk left from breakfast on my upper lip. I was immediately envious. A few of my neighbors at home raised game roosters. The roosters were beautiful but obnoxious. Those chickens came to mind every time I saw the man.

As we were finishing the treatments, a colonel from the unit we were treating came into our treatment room and was checking on his men. The medical doctor, who rarely acknowledged the presence of his own coworkers, took the colonel on a grand tour of the facility and explained the treatment of each of the wounded. He took him to the man I had ready to ship out, and I heard him ask the soldier, "Are you in any pain?" The man said, "A little."

Then, in a voice that filled the room, the medical doctor said, "I'll get you some morphine." I stood frozen on the other side of the room as the perfectly dressed doctor put morphine into the patient's left arm and walked away proudly with the colonel.

I worked my way slowly back and checked his blood pressure. There was no blood pressure. I quickly sent for Dr. Martin, and by the time Dr. Martin got to us, the man was taking his final, agonizing breaths.

We talked about the situation after the treatment room had cleared. I had, and still have, trouble believing that the doctor with the handsome mustache was not guilty of some malpractice. I had to concede that there was probably more internal damage than we knew. I still struggled with the loss of that man.

Two weeks later, the well-dressed doctor who thought so

much of himself went on R&R. I did not miss him.

When he was gone, I saw in his place an average-looking man in a medical officer's uniform, a normal haircut and no mustache.

I looked up my friend in the company clerk to ask what had happened to the doctor. It seems he had angered some PFC at the customs line at the airport and had been told to get his hair and mustache brought to military standards.

Even with my distaste for the man, it was difficult to see a colorful rooster caponized.

EXTRACTION

ONE MORNING AFTER a typical sick call session, Mr Sharpe, one of our medevac pilots, walked through the treatment area and asked, "Have you ever been on one of our extraction missions?" I had heard the words "Have you ever" a few times. What followed was never a lovely experience, but I had not been on an extraction mission, and I took the bait.

Sharpe assured me it was a simple mission, not too far from our base, and that he would take care of getting permission from my CO, but that we needed to leave "right now." "Right now" was also a red flag.

An extraction mission for the medevac crew was a mission into terrain too rugged for the helicopter to land. The crew dropped a cable with a harness, the ground troops attached the wounded man, and the helicopter crew reeled him up and took him to the aid station.

Is it ever that simple and straightforward? No. The regular medic for this crew was on board, and while I thought about it, I never asked, "Why do you need me?"

§

The flight out was beautiful. The top of the jungle is amazing, the foliage bright, rich, and peaceful. We found the pickup sight, and Mr Sharpe put the chopper in a breathless hover. I could not see the ground through the canopy, but I was sure the crew did.

The cable and harness dropped and disappeared. I got interested now and started pumping the charge medic about what we were bringing in. He said that a soldier was having a reaction to illegal drugs he had been taking and was turning himself in to a drug rehab program the Army had recently started. We were sent out because his unit feared he had OD'd, and they were afraid he would die on them before they could get to an open area.

When the man broke through the trees, I saw why I had been asked to come on the mission. The man was a canine handler, and tied to him was the biggest, meanest German Shepherd I had ever seen. I was the go-to person for treating animals on base, but this was not something I was prepared for.

The drugged soldier had a muzzle on his belt. The problem was that he was not conscious enough to put it on the dog. The dog had one purpose in life right now. He was going to make damn sure no one touched his human.

The drugged soldier was basically comatose. We tried a few things to get to the man so we could release him from the harness and get him to wake up enough to put the muzzle on his dog. I finally decided the man was not likely to die before we got back to the aid station and that if we did something dumb, the same could not be said of us. We got the man and dog mid-ship and headed quickly for home.

On the trip back, I worked on how to get the dog under control once we got to base. The whole trip, that dog looked at me with murder on his mind. There was a substantial collar on the beast and a strong lead rope on the soldier's pack, so I figured I could get one of the thick canvas tarps we had in the morgue, throw the tarp over the dog, and hold him down long enough to get the lead on him. Then I'd tie the lead to one of the tie-downs on the chopper, short enough that we could escape his bite. Then, we would release the soldier from the harness and get him to the treatment area where one of the doctors could pump enough meds into him to reverse the hold of the drugs. After that was done, we could let the soldier deal with his dog.

I called ahead so the crew could have everything ready.

We landed, and the aid station had all the equipment ready and a sizeable audience of onlookers ready to cheer on a disaster in the making. I got everything arranged like I wanted and took a deep breath.

When I threw the tarp over that dog, he exploded. I held my ground and was getting ready for the death-defying main trick of the performance when the drugged soldier woke up and said two words I had never heard before.

He calmly placed the muzzle and the lead rope on the dog, and they walked quietly into the treatment area.

Z

IN A 1969 jungle residency, mid-war, and a long way from cities of influence, serious reading material was hard to come by. Securing good current hardback fiction or historical novels was essentially impossible. Charlie Company 15th Medical Battalion in Viet Nam employed some highly-educated avid readers who used creative means to obtain books but learned to follow the "read what you can find" doctrine.

In Charlie Company, a small flock of mentally magnificent, if slightly physically challenged, medics were better than the rest of us mere mortals at finding and securing decent literature. The smart boys were also the keepers of the company day room and part-time library. I had been a member of Company C a month before I knew we had a day room, much less that the smart guys kept chess games and an assortment of other board games going constantly and maintained a library with their own book-lending system.

One of my intellectual buddies had been in the treatment room early morning and, in his effort at light conversation, mentioned that his brother had sent him a copy of V. Vassilikos' new book Z.

He had finished reading it and said I was welcome to borrow it. I did not want to sound dumb, and I had finished the stack of mediocre books in my collection, so I asked him to save it for me, I would be by to pick it up. I mentioned the title to one of the MDs working with us that morning. He laughed gently and said, "You'll never wade through it." I took that as a challenge.

After the noon chow call, I wandered over to the company day room. The one thing you could count on when walking into an unfamiliar military office was never being greeted by what you expect.

I walked into a group of slow-moving, pudgy young males loosely adorned in U.S. Army clothing. Four of them, including the lead man who had promised me the new book, were spread evenly around a dust-covered tabletop that had once been the spool for a large roll of telephone wire, all talking at once and intensely about something on the table that I could not see.

There were no books, chess tables, or even jigsaw puzzles entertaining this bunch of scholars. As I got closer, I saw a pistol being pushed tentatively from one to the other. One of the nerds had found it abandoned in the ward. These men were passing it around with the interest and excitement they would have given a toy train found unexpectedly under their Christmas tree.

They saw me walk in, and before I could panic and grab the thing, the softest member of the gang handed it to me and said, "Hey, Big Doc, you were in the field. What exactly is this?" In the blink of an eye, I went from frightened to relieved to a combat expert specializing in handguns.

Before I could rein myself in, I got all the bullets out of the weapon, explaining all the time this was a 1911 model semi-automatic, 45 cal. U.S. Army pistol. Then added in a teaching voice that this particular weapon was manufactured by Winchester, but the same pistol was made by Ruger, Colt, Stevens, and Remington and that all the parts manufactured by one of the companies would replace the same part made by one of the other companies. I quickly field-dressed the pistol and laid it out so that each part was roughly where it would fit in the weapon when reassembled. I was enjoying the attention the noncombatants were giving my show and expertise and was going into much too much detail concerning the small trigger spring when a large enemy rocket landed and exploded less than two hundred feet from us. It shook the building and day room like a rag doll in the mouth of a pitbull.

All the dust, which had been lying on the floor of the building for just this opportunity, jumped to attention. It leveled off at three feet and formed a red cloud, which returned to its home on the floor and the barely exposed parts of the four men who had been standing with me. There was a bunker at the rear of the building constructed from half of a six-foot circumstance metal culvert, the top surface covered with two layers of sandbags. The bunker was a common device to protect men under bombardment from situations like this, but it was not effective if the men involved had no warning.

I had been concerned about the mobility of these more fragile members of the medical corp, who were kept out of the excitement of combat. My worries were misplaced with this crew. When the rocket hit, I had been standing between the men and the culvert, but by the time I fully understood the situation, the whole covey of men was packed into the bunker like sardines in a zip-top tin. I considered joining them but knew instantly there was no room for my frame in the protective device.

I was still standing at the table looking at the gutted pistol, knowing that something had to be done to keep the pistol out of my friends' hands. The bullets, except the one I ejected from the cylinder, were still in their magazine on the table. I grabbed them and slammed them into my pocket, then, for good measure, took the trigger mechanism also. Then, with blind faith that no more rockets were in the air headed our way, I rushed outside.

I could see smoke in the building next door and decided to check things out there. By the time I got to the door, all my co-workers from the treatment facility were on the scene with jeep and litters. The building was the sleeping quarters for a detachment of helicopter pilots. Four of the pilots were asleep, anticipating night flights. Their roommates were flying missions. We quickly checked them all for pulse, breathing, and airway blockage. Only two of the men were responsive. We loaded them carefully and got them the short distance to the facility. There was not much hope for the remaining two, but we got them quickly to the facility, just in case.

We got the casualties undressed and inspected. One of the guys was beyond help. I moved him to the back of our treatment room, covered his remains, and promised to come back when his teammates were treated.

The three remaining injured pilots each had an MD working with him. I went from one to the other table, trying to fill a need. I brought a unit of blood to one of the medics and took a chest x-ray for one of the doctors to rule out a collapsed lung, then found gainful employ prepping the remaining man for a surgical procedure.

The pilot facing surgery was an amazing specimen of humanity. He had the clearest water-blue eyes I had ever seen. His hair was a military cut, golden blond with the sheen and shine of a summer sunrise. His face was shaved and free of blemish. His forehead, cheekbones, and chin were chiseled like the pure Italian sculptures I had seen in pictures.

The pilot was aware of the attention we were paying him but did not express any fear or, in fact, any emotion. We asked a few general questions, and he answered them with a nod or grunt. I talked him through the process of the IV I was placing in his left arm. It became obvious that the nerves I was trying to settle were mine. My pilot patient was not anxious.

Until now, I had not looked closely at the wound this Adonis had suffered. Charlie Company had one medical doctor who had served in the U.S. Army for six months in a surgical hospital in Saigon. This man had seen and performed almost all emergency medical procedures known to man. He was also blessed with the natural talent and polish of an artist. The pilot was fortunate that we had such a surgeon and that he was assigned this job.

The handsome pilot had been in his bunk when the rocket exploded. None of the metal fragments from the device hit him, but the explosion had ripped the wooden wall and ceiling beams into arrow-like projectiles that flew through the building. A sharp splintered roof fragment about five inches long had pierced his genitals and lodged them firmly into the inner aspect of his right thigh.

I looked around the room, hoping someone wanted to assist in this operation. The room was full of medical personnel much more qualified than me, but they were all suddenly very busy, had their backs to us, and were as far from our surgical table as possible.

The artist surgeon had cleaned the area around the splinter, injected the appropriate skin, prepped the field, gloved, and was motioning for me to open his surgical pack, glove myself, and help him. He attacked the wound so gently, sweetly, and quickly that I was hard-pressed to keep the man supplied with instruments while suturing and keeping the field clean of unwanted debris. He got the wooden parts out of the pilot and flushed the exposed area with saline water, then closed the parts of the wound he knew would heal without more treatment. He checked the genital wound to make sure there was no bleeding. After assuring himself he had things as stable as possible, he bandaged the damaged area and left me to clean up while he went to make sure the transport helicopter was en route. He wrote orders to the receiving hospital facility.

I looked again into the face of the pilot. His expression had not changed. If the man was concerned about his condition or future, he hid it well. I wanted to talk to him but could not. The super surgeon came back to us by the time I had the patient covered and ready to transport. The doctor was not as constrained. He asked the pilot how he felt and if he had any questions. My pilot patient broke his silence and asked, "Will I be able to fly?"

The surgeon measured the pilot slowly from head to toe and, in his own bedside manner, said, "I can't see any reason you won't recover and resume your flight duties." Then, after a pause, he said, "And in case you're wondering, you should also be able to father many children."

I looked for a sign that he was relieved by the fatherhood statement. There was none. We loaded the pilot almost immediately onto a just-arrived helicopter, and he was off to a hospital in Saigon.

The experienced hands of Charlie Company's treatment room had the facility back to the ready-for-new-casualties position. I went back to the day room to check on my book and the status of the pistol.

When I walked in, the head ward nurse was alone, writing letters. We talked briefly about the wounded pilots. He gave me the pistol to dispose of properly and handed me the book.

The events surrounding the 1963 Greek assassination were not especially interesting, and the characters in the historical novel were not likable, but I slogged through the entire thing. It took a week and several vacations to more agreeable reading, but I finished it and took every advantage of the bragging rights I was due for doing so.

MAJOR STONE

AFTER THE CLOSE of the Cambodian May of 1970, just after the gaudy inventory of weapons and ammo we captured, and just before the avalanche of malaria cases in our soldiers who invaded that country, enemy activity came to a halt. The 7th Cav found itself with nothing warlike to do. To make things worse, the base camp was invaded and occupied by the local Infantry Division of South Vietnamese Regulars. We had so many boots on the ground carrying loaded weapons that it was dangerous to walk to the outhouse.

The U.S. Army is fully prepared to handle such problems and found an unoccupied base camp east of Saigon called Bear Cat or some name similar. It had previously been the home of a French military outfit and was recently used by a unit of the U.S. Army's 25th Infantry. The 7th Cav was ordered to take over the base and go back to making war with the Viet Cong and NVA. For reasons known only to the Gods of War, I was assigned to accompany two medical doctors—captains of the Medical Corp—and a fellow medical aid man as advance party for the company. I was to set up and operate a treatment facility there until the main company could pack its many bags and move to us.

We arrived to find a deserted base camp. We stopped at the main entrance to report to a dirty PFC and found the peace instantly broken by a rhythmic and regular loud explosion followed by a 10-foot-high pillar of dust. When the dust settled, it became clear that the noise and dirt bomb were somehow related to a large bulldozer sitting idly as the dust slowly covered it. The big machine was systematically clearing landmines in the empty field to the right of the main entrance. We heard stories from many sources, some

David Rozzell

reliable, that the French occupier had left landmines everywhere around the base perimeter. We were ahead of schedule and watched longer than was necessary as the driver of that dozer went about his business. He would drive as straight as planting corn rows back home until he ran over one of those mines. There would be a big explosion and lots of dirt. The dirt would settle. The driver would shake his head, get out on the hood of the dozer, take his earplugs out and wipe them off, replace them, then get back in the big piece of equipment and repeat the exercise. I never set foot outside the perimeter of that base camp.

The PFC at the main gate called a high-level buck sergeant, who escorted us to our new billets and aid station. He left us to our own devices. The treatment building had recently housed the Headquarters Company of the 25th Infantry and was in good repair. We set up what basic equipment we had, ran our flag up outside, and awaited business.

There was an outbuilding behind the treatment facility. It had been the officer barracks, but since there were only four of us, we moved in together. One of the officers who deserted the barracks must have had home in the U.S. as his next duty assignment. He left behind three new uniforms. The uniforms fit me, so I took immediate possession of them.

All three of the uniforms were officer quality. They had never been worn. They were hung from a nail in the back of the barrack in individual opaque plastic bags, each sealed at the bottom to prevent the entry of offensive dust. The hangers were white plastic-coated metal and did not have a hint of rust. The uniforms were not just clean, they were pristine. The name and insignia were also works of art.

My coworkers showed no interest in the prize, so in times of marginal official business, I was Major Stone, and I looked good. I did sometimes wear one of the vestments, at times verging on a dangerous violation like impersonating an officer. It was a neat feeling to have soldiers salute me and come into the office expecting me to help them more skillfully than the lower-ranking members of my team. But it was also a bogus feeling, and I was never sure I enjoyed it.

The 7th Cav was in a new area of operation, and fortunately, it took a few days for them to find serious military activity and give us gainful employment. Sick call was another story. There was never a shortage of minor medical needs at a military facility. At this work site, there were new places offering the favorite pleasures sought by young men with too much time on their hands, and until the unhealthy providers had been culled, we had a steady flow of men with sexually transmitted diseases. With the full complement of a medical company, this problem and the exact disease were routinely discovered by sending a little blood to the lab and waiting 20 min or so for the tech to process the sample and tell us what the problem was and what was the appropriate drug of choice.

We had no lab tech. We solved the problem in an informal council of war the afternoon of the second day. We took a basic and direct approach. It did not take a detective to know which guys were suffering the effects. The man would be wearing his boonie hat pulled down over his eyes and, when approached, would turn sideways and mumble, "Doc, I got a drip." Our new diagnostic tool was a question. "What color is the drip?" It was amazing the graphic, vivid, and imaginative descriptions a common foot soldier can give that question. The diagnosis, no matter the color, was the same. We looked the man squarely in the eyes and, with the best fatherly voice we could muster, assured the guy he had a case of the "Clap." Then, we assured him that a few rounds of penicillin would solve the problem. A short lecture always followed the first injection of a painful antibiotic, and the penitent warrior left, swearing never to let it happen again.

In what seemed like forever and no time at all, the real 15th Medical Company arrived. The base camp was becoming populated with angry-looking military personnel. Casualties of war filled our aid facility. One not-so-well-meaning sergeant who outranked me slightly had heard of my officer ambitions and threatened to have me

David Rozzell

brought up on charges if he ever heard of me wearing the uniforms in question. I lovingly packed away my uniforms and went about the work as usual.

A week or so after we had the new facility up and in full production, a young private limped into the treatment area around midday. He had twisted his ankle severely and had some cuts and bumps he had suffered in the accident. The youngster had no military carriage and looked to be fifteen years of age. He was not much into shaving.

It was a busy day, and our medevac helicopters were getting more work than usual. I cleaned up and bandaged his easy wounds and got admission papers fixed up for the youngster to enter the evac hospital for more treatment. I set him in the waiting area for shipment on the next helicopter going out. The next chopper came and went. My boy was overlooked. He was not standing up for himself, and I didn't pay much attention to the matter. A second helicopter came and left him slumped in the same spot at the end of our waiting bench. That really bothered me. I quickly went to my trunk and brought out Major Stone. I quietly removed the torn, grease-smeared uniform from the kid's back and gently eased him into his new rank. When the next supply chopper came, I made sure he boarded and was treated with respect.

No one in our company commented on the incident. The boy did nothing wrong. All the kid's paperwork carried the private first-class words. Somebody had seen how dirty his uniform top was and put a clean one on him.

The young man came back to our base camp a month or so later and was fine. He went back to his job and worked full shifts in the 7th Cav Motor Pool. He came by the treatment office late one afternoon to give me an update on his injury. He made a point to thank me for the uniform. The treatment men at the evac hospital had come to meet him with a wheelchair and treated him like royalty. He was never sure at what point they realized he was a PFC, but he got good treatment during his entire stay.

PATTON

AFTER A MORNING of setting up our new temporary aid station, Dr. Martin and I took a walk around the new base camp. There was a small contingent of military police, a helicopter land pad under construction, and a battalion headquarters facility. It was dusty and hot, but we had no other duties, so we were exploring.

The only person we saw all morning was a rather large human in the rear of the headquarters building. He was shirtless and carrying on an animated conversation, but we could neither hear nor see who he may have been talking to. We could clearly see he had a pearl-handled revolver holstered on each hip in Roy Rogers fashion.

After finding nothing else unusual or interesting, we started walking back to our new workstation. As we walked a street below the headquarters, a Loach helicopter flew overhead and hovered over the steps of the headquarters building. It sat there for a minute and then appeared to drop a body onto the porch of the building. Martin and I exchanged looks and decided that whatever this was, it was none of our business.

The Army held a "war meeting" every afternoon, and the ranking member of each group on base was required to attend. Dr. Martin was now our ranking member, so he did his duty. The other two members of our company started a high-stakes poker game.

An hour or so later, Dr. Martin returned. He took his seat at the poker table with the twenty matches we used as poker chips. After a few hands, I asked how his meeting had gone. He mumbled that it was just the usual boring gathering. Then he mentioned the incident of the VC being dropped on the headquarters porch.

That morning, the helicopter bunch had called in that they had found and killed a high-level VC and wanted to know how to handle the credit. The colonel had personally gotten on the radio and told them to "drop the body on his doorstep." As Martin and I knew, they had done so.

The story did not end there. The colonel got even more irate and called the pilots back with orders to "get that body off his porch and dump it in the jungle." The pilots did so, thinking that ended the event. It didn't. Someone higher up the food chain with General for a first name heard about the incident.

Why military men of whatever rank do what they do is beyond me, but the general decided the colonel had done something bad. The general personally ordered the same pilot to find the VC's body, bring it back to his headquarters, and make sure it was given a proper burial. The pilot did not find this task as easy but managed to do it.

The general relieved the colonel of his command and reassigned him to a job in the States. Dr. Martin told us the rumor at the war meeting was that the colonel had been treated unkindly because he was the son of George Patton.

At this point, we were all ready to get on with the poker game. We were all students of military history, and we did not believe that George Patton had a son, much less one in the service or in Vietnam.

THE GAZE

LATE ONE MORNING, after we had finished sick call and before the daily rain came, the 11th A Cav got hit by a sniper and asked for a medevac to take out a couple of wounded. They were not far away, and the crew was back quickly.

There were three wounded. Only one was on a litter, and the other two walked with help. One of the walking wounded had taken two rounds in the upper part of his left arm. The third man had a big general-purpose bandage firmly attached to his forehead. His vital signs were good, so we sat him on a bench until we treated the other men.

The man on the litter had a chest wound but was stable. Dr. Martin cleaned the wound and, with sucking chest wound protocol, bandaged him.

The man with the arm wounds took more time to clean up and bandage, but it was routine.

I started paperwork on the men and had the clerk request transport to the evac hospital. When I finished that task, I went to help Dr. Martin with the last patient, who was seated upright on our first treatment litter. He had taken the oversized bandage off but was just looking at the man's forehead.

When I got beside Dr. Martin, I knew the reason for his quiet. Behind the oversized bandage, the young man had a hole dead center on his forehead. I was stunned to my core. Martin and I never exchanged looks or words. He had an instrument pack laid out and, from it, took a probe and gently explored the edges of the wound. There were no other marks on the man's body. The thought of an x-ray occurred to me, but I left it there.

The man had shown no emotion or made sounds of any kind since arriving. I made eye contact with the man, and it was the most haunting experience of my life. Everything that suggested human life was missing from his blank gaze, yet he walked normally when directed.

The message of that gaze, coupled with the unmistakable meaning of the perfect round wound always in the view of those eyes, was otherworldly. I saw many horrible things in the treatment of battle wounded. Some I have been able to write about, all come back to my dreams occasionally, but this is the only event that comes into my thoughts every day.

I stayed by the man's side until the helicopter transport appeared. Once he was safely on the helicopter, I went back to my station. I was near Dr. Martin the rest of the day. We talked as usual, but there was never mention of the forehead wound, the patient he and I alone shared.

FINAL EXAM

THAT MORNING, THE sick call line was led by Billy, a meek, undersized, eighteen-year-old PFC who served as a rifleman in the 1st squad of Bravo Company, 8th Brigade, 1st Cavalry Division. The unit was headquartered a few doors west of our aid facility. For the two weeks leading up to this morning, his squad had been involved in some heavy combat situations. The unit was an air-mobile unit of the "bring you in when fighting is really bad, and we need more guns" kind. When times were good, they spent most of their time training a few hours a day and then hanging out at the PX or one of the many continuous card games on base. The last month, their card games had been shorter than usual, and the 1st squad had been emptying a lot of ammo boxes.

Billy was never a rock star soldier. He would take any opportunity or reason to avoid a gunfight, so we knew him pretty well. His medical file was easily the thickest we had in our facility. In the two weeks of his squad's heaviest action, Billy had been an early morning regular. We knew his history and knew his unit was on base. He came to my desk with the same general symptoms and with the same pitiful attitude. He said he was sick all over and had a fever and just had no energy.

As a human being, Billy was not of the angry, cursing, demanding type. I never heard him say, or heard of him saying, we were "treating him unfairly" or "picking on him." We had tested everything we had equipment to check, and our best medical doctors had physically checked him. At this point, we, as a medical body, were convinced that Billy was a garden variety "gold brick" soldier. Following the visit Billy had paid us just two days ago, we called his platoon leader in and explained that we could find no reason he should not be returned to duty. The highest-ranking doctor of our unit had signed papers to that effect, and we washed our hands of the affair.

Billy showed a lot of persistence and ability to absorb abuse coming back to see us again, and for that reason alone, I took some blood from him along with the blood pressure, pulse, respiration, and temperature routine for such visits. When everything turned up normal, I sent him back to his unit.

The morning went routinely for an hour or so, and then the medical tech walked in. He had just finished the blood workup, and Billy was positively suffering from malaria.

The work staff held a short meeting and decided that since I was the medic who last treated Billy, it was only fair that I take the news to him and his commanding officer. Ever the good little soldier and the low-ranking member, I picked up the revised paperwork and headed west to Billy's company headquarters. The top sergeant was not happy to see me or hear my news, but he quickly got word to Billy's squad leader to replace him and send him to headquarters.

I stood around uncomfortably in the dust and heat of the headquarters office, expecting to have a long wait. I was surprised that Billy appeared almost immediately. The company was in their jeep, ready to leave for the land strip, and Billy got what he called a stay of execution. I explained what had happened and that we needed him back at our treatment facility to start meds and hospitalization immediately. He did not seem surprised and gave me the "I told you I was sick" look.

I got Billy signed into the ward just in time to make it to the mess hall before last call. The cook squad pushed me hard to finish so they could get out of the kitchen. I rushed through the mystery meat of the day and went back to the treatment facility.

The rest of the day was uneventful. I got a couple of surgical packs sorted, swept the floor a few times, and read an interesting chapter of *The Merck Manual* concerning antibiotic treatment for urinary tract infections. Just before evening chow, a medevac chopper came in and dropped us a gunshot victim. The poor soldier was showing a newbie how to safely clean an M16 rifle when it discharged a round through his right foot. It took little time to clean it up and send him off to the bigger hospital. As I was leaving for chow, the company clerk met me and walked to mess with me.

Once we were seated, the clerk surprised me. He had just gotten paperwork that I was listed to process out-of-country the next morning and to report to Bien Hoa airport by late the next afternoon in preparation for returning home. My short-timer calendar still showed two weeks before I was due to leave. We made small talk, ate our meals, and made plans for me to meet him at the company headquarters at 1900 hours to start the paperwork. I did not remember eating anything.

For an undertaking as complicated as moving a soldier from one military unit to another and then miles and miles to his home, the paperwork required was child's play. My clerk handed me a single sheet of paper with a listing of the company subsection spelled out and a block at the far right side of the paper that the department boss initialed, saying I turned in all the equipment I had borrowed, used, and worn. I knew the head of each branch and quickly ran each down and had them initial my paper. The medical was a bit more involved, but since I usually performed the physical for each of the men leaving, I did a windshield evaluation, filled in the blanks, initialed the sheet, and moved on. In less than 30 minutes, I had the papers complete with the necessary autographs and back to the clerk's office. He was to get the commanding officer's approval the next morning, and I would be good to go.

I did not even pretend I would be able to sleep. I packed up all the things I wanted to take home with me, and they filled only the bottom of my duffel bag. I dumped a clean pair of underwear, a pair of socks, and a *Merck Manual* I had rescued from book heaven. The remaining hoard I got in a heap between my bunk and the hutch door. I can't remember a complete inventory, but there were a few underpants and shirts that had never been worn. There was a pair of jungle boots that were highly polished and never worn. There were at least two sets of fatigue uniforms, still in the condition they came from supply. I had a stack of books I had traded or borrowed against hard times and a reel-to-reel tape recorder, which I had inherited from a roommate who did not want to take it home with him.

When morning broke, I dressed smartly and sat numbly on my bunk until I could hear daily life outside the hootch. I went out to breakfast and ate quickly. I was aware that I was not included in the chatter of the morning but not alive enough to think anything of it. I shuffled back to my little room and found my roommates had gone to their duty stations without me. I methodically marshaled my worldly possessions to the left side of my hootch door, gathered up my near-empty duffel bag and necessary paperwork, and walked toward the office without looking back.

At the company office, my clerk friend took the remaining indispensable papers to the commanding officer, who signed them without comment or a glance to see who they were for. I was ushered out the door and told to meet the resupply helicopter, which would be leaving for Bien Hoa shortly. I knew it would be half an hour easily before departure and thought I would like to see the treatment facility one last time.

Sick call was over for the morning and the crew was cleaning the treatment room and discussing the morning events. I walked through the door expecting some congratulations, good luck speeches, "We'll sure miss you around here," or some social banter. No one seemed to notice I was there. I walked a bit closer and shuffled my feet a little, but still got no reaction. At this point, I figured the guys were playing with my mind, and if I turned to leave, they would bring me back and give the old family send-off. So, I turned and walked slowly towards the door and the helicopter that was now awaiting resupply. There was no comment, and when the helicopter was in the air and the company area out of sight, I was left with the feeling of just having attended my own funeral.

HOME

OFF A DUSTY mud-red, steep, and weedless drive, veiled by low-hanging branches, across a creek, playing the song it learned with the Earth's first raindrops. Music flushed from rubbing leaves, limbs, and stones of the stream banks. A changing wind adds harmony to the melody.

The sweet smell of fresh-cut grass was tempered by the stench of the decaying mound of the season's clippings.

White to gray plumes of chimney smoke's promising and crackling low tune. Bright soothing colors moving to the same music. The smell of oak, pine, and poplar wood smoldering, cheerfully giving seasoned fruit of many years struggle to my comfort.

A fortress of thick walls slows the attacking goodwill of the well-meaning world. Holding my fears in a safe circle of tempered glue. A fragile security.

A mother's long-suffering and acceptance. A few yards short of understanding, miles past any necessity/duty/expectation. A life's mission to assure peace and harmony in the ranks of her charge.

A father's never-ending love affair with all things competitive. Any contest pitting two or more people in games involving a stick and ball, man testing men. Bragging rights always the ultimate prize. Always holding the sport, the game, the contest more important than the score.

Then, the visits. Neighbors, family, extended family, friends, schoolmates, church family. All are interested. None speak a language in which I am any longer fluent. All still holding to a tongue we shared before I left. What is left of me is a cold and dimly lit painting displayed in a gallery: "Doesn't he look fit, trim, healthy."

Home from an ugly war, my body healthy, mind and soul a mess. I returned to work, no questions where I'd been. Working constantly to numb the horror.

What remains is a long, slow, and painful reeducation for my blistered soul, a cradle for my wandering mind, shuffling among strangers who were, and are now again, my fellow man.

ACKNOWLEDGMENTS

David Thomas Rozzell – Deceased October 22, 2022

We would like to express our profound gratitude to Joseph Bathanti for his impact on David's writing. In 2014, Joseph assumed the role of Charles George VA Medical Center Writer-In-Residence. Along with Dr. Bruce Kelly, he launched a writing program for Vietnam combat veterans. This safe, nonjudgmental environment created a zone where David found his voice and knew that he was not alone. Thank you, Joseph, for helping David find his remarkable gift of writing.

We would like to express our profound gratitude to Dr. Bruce Kelly, Charles George VA Medical Center, for recognizing that the Vietnam combat veterans need mental healing as well as physical healing. This transferred the face of what healing looks like. Dr. Kelly, along with Joseph Bathanti and cohorts of Vietnam veterans, started meeting in Classroom B, and the results were overwhelmingly positive. Dr. Kelly, thank you for helping David find his voice and his way in society again.

We would like to express our profound gratitude to David's niece, Jody Brooks, English Professor at Georgia State University. She and her Uncle David had a close and loving relationship, and they discussed their ideas for writing future stories. David shared his goals for the publication of his Vietnam stories, and Jody has kept her promise to share his voice. Thank you, Jody, for proofreading, editing, pruning, and overall supervision of every detail of this book.

We would like to honor David's parents, Grady and Betty Rozzell. Their love and support for David were unconditional, and David loved them immensely.

Finally, we believe David would have predicted that his wife, Judy, and his three Baby Sisters, Terri, Carol, and Pegg, would eagerly entrust the role of support staff to Jody. Special thanks to Joe Brooks for collecting David's stories, which resided on three laptops. The drill started with "Does anyone know his password?"

Thanks to the entire support team.

Acknowledgments were made by David's sisters, Terri Rozzell Brooks, Carol Rozzell Tyson, and Pegg Rozzell, who loved him dearly.

Uncle David

He could hit a golf ball to the great beyond
and shared his wisdom on the velvet greens.
Proud as we picked up rackets, bats, clubs and beat
our opponents with finesse. "Feel the rhythm," he said
when we got too far in our heads. "You'll be fine," he said
when our bodies ached. "Just don't slow down."

Ben the Beagle, Wolfpack pride,
blue ribbons, trophies, horseshoes.
Animals who heal and are healed
by his powerful hands. The rich
smell of earth, a weathered barn.
Horses calm in his presence.

Viking blood coursing through gentle hands.
Foreign strangers turned friends, the language of kindness breaks
barriers. He traced us back to royalty, but we didn't need proof
of his dignity, his honor, his noble stature.

A patient physician, good and true.
A warm, hearty baritone, poet and scholar,
authentic, perceptive, skilled.
Who wouldn't love brothers like these?

Resolve of steel and copper padlocks,
the inveterate shadows locked behind screen doors.
We must all brave the inevitable parting, the final mission, healing
as chains fall away, light as air, quiet, peaceful.

When the sun sets and the stars bronze, we will remember you.
Stand down, rest easy. You travel now with us.

–Jody Brooks, 2022

David Thomas Rozzell
February 23, 1946—October 22, 2022

David had a long and troubled journey but never stopped loving and longing for all that was good. He was a man without prejudice, and he loved without judgment.

PERMISSIONS

"Final Exam" first appeared in Kelly, Richard, and Elizabeth Heaney. *Brothers & Sisters like These: An Anthology of Writing by Veterans*. Redhawk Publications, the Catawba Valley Community College Press, 2023.

"Purple" first appeared as "Evasive Measures." Marshall, Dan, and Jody Brooks, editors. *gsu review,* Fall 2004.

"What Healing Looks Like" first appeared in Bathanti, Joseph, et al. *Brothers like These: Vietnam War Veterans: Poems & Prose*. St. Andrews University Press, 2017.

"Christmas Eve" first appeared as "Music From the Sky" in Bathanti, Joseph, et al. *Brothers like These: Vietnam War Veterans: Poems & Prose*. St. Andrews University Press, 2017.

"Home" forthcoming in new anthology

"Bob" forthcoming in new anthology

Made in the USA
Middletown, DE
02 May 2025

74938998R00128